PITCH THE BITCH

Grab your financial future by the bags

KELLY ANN WINGET

DIVERSITY CREW
PRESS

www.DiversityCrewPress.com

To book Kelly Ann Winget for interviews or speaking
please email LetsGo@DiversityCrew.com

ISBN 978-1-66789-236-8

DIVERSITY CREW
PRESS

To all of the strong, independent women in my life, especially my wife, my sister, and my mother. Thank you for supporting me through the up and down markets of life.

Contents

INTRODUCTION

My very first job was at a car wash. At fifteen years old, I was the only female employee, surrounded by dirty cars, large machinery, sponges, rags, teenage boys, and men. Since then, until I went out on my own, not much had changed except the industry where I worked. I moved on to jobs in construction and finance. Eventually, I became the director of investor relations at an independent oil and gas firm in North Dallas. I've always worked in sales, and I've always been surrounded by men.

But that wasn't the problem per se. At the last firm where I worked, I attained my aspirations, but I still didn't feel like I was doing what I wanted to do. Something was nagging at me.

Like for so many others, 2020 was a time to reflect and a time to make a change for the better.

Over the years, I learned that financial companies don't treat women the same way they treat men. Most major decisions made at the bigger firms are made by senior partners—i.e., sixty—plus-year-old white guys who have been in the business for decades. I noticed that when working with heterosexual married couples, financial advisors prioritize the husbands, which I find ironic because, in most cases, the wives are the ones to run the household finances. The wives run the budget, write the checks, and make a ton of decisions that affect the family's finances. They take care of all of it. Except investing.

If you're reading this book, you're probably a woman, and I have bad news for you: Unless you're the rare exception, your financial advisor doesn't care about you. Statistics show that nearly 80 percent of women change financial advisors after their husbands die because the advisor doesn't treat her the same way they treated her husband. When they see how little attention they get compared to the way their husbands were treated, they make tracks.

My mother has had a female financial advisor for forever, and she's very happy with her. The woman actually *sees* my mother and her needs and priorities. It's a great relationship. But finding a female financial advisor is hard—so few exist. If you can find one, you will typically find she cares more, and that you're not just a number to her.

Of course, these statements are broad generalizations, but like all generalizations, there's a reason for them. They hold true in part because financial advisors don't really care about their clients at all, male or female. The majority of American financial advisors are not actively engaged. For your managed portfolio, they select one of three funds based on your risk tolerance: Fund A, a conservative fund; Fund B, for the moderate risk-taker; or Fund C, the aggressive choice. And that's what the account will look like for the rest of your life. No one is really paying attention. ***No one cares all that much about your money besides you.***

The thing is, there are so many other options out there. But to most people, they're not accessible. Private equity is intentionally mysterious in order to remain exclusive. For those who don't qualify as "accredited investors"—those who have a net worth of at least $1 million without including their home as an asset or someone who makes $200,000+ annually—it seems like there are no good opportunities beyond real estate, where there's no barrier to entry. But, in fact, there are other options, and this book is the reader's key to a world of investing that has traditionally been locked away. When I was a teenager, I made $60,000 working part-time selling car detailing services. I made over $200,000 as a twenty-four-year-old consultant, making me an accredited investor before I was twenty-five. As a result, my fear of sales and entrepreneurship is pretty much nonexistent, and it taught me that I could make money doing just about anything I chose. And so can you.

Today, I call myself a contrarian, which has a specific meaning in the investment world, i.e., when everyone else is doing one thing, I do the other. So, in 2020, when investors were wringing their hands about the state of their portfolios and the media was gushing news about the wildly fluctuating stock market, I took a risk. And I'm glad I did.

I founded a Private Equity Firm, Alternative Wealth Partners (AWP), to provide access to digestible information about alternative investments and educate investors about the opportunities available off Wall Street. After all, since the financial crash of 2008, I have been aggressively connecting creative capital to unique investment opportunities in the private equity space. Through that experience, I established a vast network of relationships in multiple industries. While everyone panicked—for good reason—about their traditional investments, I could expertly source alternative investments that gave investors unmatched access to real returns. I wanted to help my clients learn how to do as well as I have and more. Together, we'd be unstoppable.

This book is for women who want to have financial independence, women interested in working in the financial services industry, women interested in launching their own company, and investors interested in looking beyond real estate syndication for real wealth generation.

With my model, I don't make money unless you, the investor, make money. My earnings are completely performance-based, so our interests are aligned. If someone is seeing an 8% return on investment with a large financial company like Edward Jones or Charles Schwab, for example, that's after fees, overhead, etc. That means your investments are earning about 25 to 30%, but you're not seeing that kind of return at all due to all the costs and fees. Everyone else gets paid before the investor.

If you're okay with 8%, this book is not for you.

If you want to take more control of your financial future, then, it is.

You're worth it. Come on this journey with me and learn how you can independently improve your finances by defining your goals and being in better investments. I mean, really, who else is going to do it? After everything we've witnessed happening on Wall Street over the past couple of decades, certainly you wouldn't trust them to take care of you.

You may ask: Why for women? I've been a feminist for my entire life. In my mind, being a feminist means believing that women deserve the same opportunities as men, whether it's in education, sports, work, or personal life. It's time someone made sure women got the same opportunities in investing.

In the pages to follow, I'll share stories of how women as investors are routinely ignored by the vast financial moneymaking machine, how women working within that machine are undervalued and overworked, and why it is so important for women to work with women when it comes to increasing wealth. I'm not the one to sugarcoat things, so I hope you're wearing your big girl pants; I'm about to throw down some hard truths. But it is my sincere hope that this book will be just the kick in the ass that you need to take ownership of your financial well-being.

The financial industry thinks that most women don't need to understand the complex mechanisms at play when it comes to generating massive wealth. Help me prove them wrong and grab your financial future by the *bags.*

CHAPTER ONE

The Myth of "Don't Pitch the Bitch"

In the 2000 American crime drama *Boiler Room*, protagonist Seth Davis lands what he thinks is a great entry job as a stockbroker trainee. During orientation, senior broker Greg Weinstein gives him what he considers standard advice: "Now, there's two rules you have to remember as a trainee. Number one, we don't pitch the bitch here."

Davis, confused, answers, "What?"

Weinstein explains, "We don't sell stock to women. I don't care who it is, we don't do it. Nancy Sinatra calls, you tell her you're sorry. They're a constant pain in the ass and you're never going to hear the end of it, all right?"

Davis looks at Weinstein, incredulous.

"They're going to call you every fucking day wanting to know why the stock is dropping," Weinstein continues. "And God forbid the stock should go up, you're going to hear from them every fucking fifteen minutes. It's just not worth it. Don't pitch the bitch."

I understand why Davis was incredulous—the first time I heard the phrase used in my presence, back in 2013, that was exactly how I felt. It was shocking that such a backward slogan was still circulating among *respectable* finance professionals (respectable being the term in question, of course). But the guy who said it had three daughters. Even if he was making a joke—and to be fair, everyone in the room was laughing—it wasn't funny. We weren't in a movie. I wasn't about to call him on it because he was one of the three owners of the company.

The room itself was a parody of the Olde Boys Club. I'd been around oil and gas companies for years, and this one was typical: stuffy, heavy oak furniture, gaudy paintings everywhere, and a unique touch—fish tanks. That place had fish tanks in every room, and these weren't just ordinary fish tanks. They were $150,000+ fish tanks stocked with aquatic creatures that went for more than $1,000 each at the exotic fish store that one of the company's partners owned. Those fish tanks were my next clue that something wasn't quite right at the firm.

There were several weekends when one of those expensive fish would jump out of the tank, and on Monday, it would be lying dead on the floor. I didn't know if the guy forgot to close the tank or if the tank was just the wrong size or what, but every Monday, another stinking dead fish appeared. And then, there'd be a new one, exactly like the one that had just jumped to his death. And this went on for weeks. I thought, *this has to be the silliest place I've ever been.*

It was my first time working with an oil & gas investment company. My job was to funnel the sales team a list of investors, run reports on what was and was not working in their own boiler room—no different, really, from the one in the movie—and then, develop teams based on their closing skills. You know, if Sam in sales took the first cold call and then tossed it to Mark the manager, who passed it on to Chris, the closer, and all together they had a 90 percent average of closing a deal, then that was a great team.

The sales happened in an honest-to-God boiler room not that different from the one in the movie. A group of guys sat around cold calling all day, selling mineral rights. The price of oil had skyrocketed, and mineral rights were an easy sell. Even though I was new there, I wasn't new to the industry. I knew the price of oil was going to fall, and it wasn't going to work out for the investors in the long-term.

I'd worked in marketing and sales before, but this was my first-time raising capital. But when I see something that's wrong, I have a hard time leaving it alone. I trusted my instincts. Something *was* wrong. *Very wrong.* So, I asked some questions, but they didn't want me asking questions, they wanted me to make baseball cards with statistics about the salespeople.

So, they let me go.

Soon enough, the price per barrel of oil plummeted. When it hit $40 a barrel, that company closed. The owners with the "don't pitch the bitch" remark? They set up an office out of the back of the exotic fish store.

That kind of thing made me realize I'd be better off opening my own business. But I wasn't quite ready yet.

Over the next several years, I ran into different situations. I consulted on investor relations, capital raising, deal structure and operations for companies with "the next best thing since sliced bread" in tech, real estate, medical devices, energy, etc. The personalities behind most of these companies weren't for the weak-hearted. They were crude, delusional and closed-minded. But boys will be boys, and they raised a lot of money… from boys.

They weren't all bad. One firm was run by someone I still admire today. He was raised by a single mother, had daughters and granddaughters, he got it. He could be difficult—some called him abrasive, and they wouldn't be wrong—but he was smart, and his largest, most loyal investors were women. I learned a lot from him. The problem there was that we were too alike to work together, he told me I needed my own firm and my own fund. He wasn't wrong, but I wasn't quite ready.

The Bitch is Winning

Here's a little-known fact: Studies show that women get better investment returns than men.

In 2021, Fidelity Investments (the fifth largest investment company in the world) sponsored a thorough study of women investors, which was completed by an independent research firm. The summary in the report stated that over a ten-year period, female investors earned, on average, 0.4 percentage points more annually than their male counterparts.[1] *The New York Times* reacted this way: "That may not seem like a lot, but over a few decades it can add up to tens of thousands of dollars or more."[2] The *Times* theorized that one reason is that men fall victim to overconfidence, whereas women investors are more cautious.[3]

Lorna Kapusta, then head of women investors and customer engagement at Fidelity, responded that the lesson is to "invest like a woman."

According to the research, women's superior returns are due to the way they trade—less frequently. In the study of 2400 investors, half female

1 https://www.fidelity.com/bin-public/060_www_fidelity_com/documents/about-fidelity/FidelityInvestmentsWomen&InvestingStudy2021.pdf
2 https://www.nytimes.com/2021/10/29/your-money/women-investing-stocks.html
3 Ibid.

and half male, the women bought and sold 50 percent less than the male investors. Vanguard discovered a similar pattern over the same ten years, involving retirement accounts: at least 50 percent more men traded in them than women did every year during that time.

Frequent trades simply don't result in strong returns, as proven in 2000 by Brad M. Barber and Terrance Odean, two professors at, respectively, the Graduate School of Management, University of California (UC) Davis, and the Haas School of Business at UC Berkeley. In the period they studied, 1991 to 1996, those who traded the most earned annual returns of 6.5 percent less than the stock market overall.

Individual investors who hold common stocks directly pay a tremendous performance penalty for active trading. Of 66,465 households with accounts at a large discount broker from 1991 to 1996, those that traded most earned an annual return of 11.4 percent, while the market returned 17.9 percent.[4]

Their conclusions? "Overconfidence can explain high trading levels and the resulting poor performance of individual investors. Our central message is that trading is hazardous to your wealth."[5]

The following year, Professors Barber and Odean addressed gender and investing habits in a different paper, this one entitled "*Boys Will Be Boys*." They learned in their research that from 1991 to 1997, women also traded more frequently than was wise, i.e., their trading resulted in net returns that were lower by 1.72 percentage points per year compared to the

4 https://faculty.haas.berkeley.edu/odean/papers%20current%20versions/individual_investor_performance_final.pdf
5 Ibid.

overall market. However, men suffered by 2.65 percentage points over the same period.[6]

The problem? According to William J. Bernstein, a neurologist who studied what could be termed the "*Boys Will Be Boys*" effect, it's testosterone, which makes men less risk averse. In other words, testosterone grows muscle mass, but shrinks investment returns.

On the other hand, women could use a little extra confidence. Fidelity surveys showed in 2017 that only 9 percent of women believed they could do better than men as investors, and in 2021, only 14 percent of women expressed confidence regarding saving and investing. Despite doing better than their male counterparts, a full two-thirds of the female respondents in the 2021 survey described being anxious and hesitant when making investment decisions.

Historically, it's been assumed that women make the budgets and men make the investments, perhaps because they were the primary earners or just felt better suited to the task. Also, the predominantly white male financial industry connected with husbands and paid little, if any, attention to wives. But more cautious investing may also stem from the fact that women are conditioned by society to be perfect, never measuring up to unrealistic standards, the last thing a woman needs is for her husband to blame her for poor investment results. Or she has a different goal—more on that in Chapter Two.

Or it could be one more holdover from Larry Summers's unfortunate 2005 claim that, for biological reasons, girls just aren't good at math. That statement may have cost him the presidency at Harvard, but it sure didn't

6 http://faculty.haas.berkeley.edu/odean/papers%20current%20versions/boyswillbeboys.pdf

hurt his reputation overall. Indeed, his experience is just one more piece of evidence that it's still a man's world. Imagine his successor at Harvard, Drew Faust—the first woman president of Harvard, by the way—suggesting that men are no good at investing, even if she had the data to prove it! Am I right? Career done in that split second. And Larry Summers gets fêted as Sheryl Sandburg's mentor and becomes Secretary of the US Treasury. It's unbelievable.

Still, we don't want to make the same mistake Summers did by relying on gender stereotypes of a bold male investor and a timid female one. Of course, there are plenty of underconfident men and fearless women on the market. All you need to do is look at Cathie Wood. Wood, if you don't know, is a veteran money manager who, tired of being told to be quiet by her male peers, founded Ark Invest and hasn't stopped since. She's a regular on all the social media and every financial news show, is usually the only woman among the talking heads, and has no trouble telling the boys they're flat wrong. Even though she's a conservative sixty-something, millennial investors hang on her every utterance.

I'm only sharing what have been identified as reliable trends and making the point that women have been made to feel less confident as investors. I've seen it myself, and the studies confirm it. And I'm sharing that ironically, it can pay off; women who resist bailing on stocks that are falling and hang tight through market upheavals inevitably see better results.

There's an irony in this gender stereotyping. Men who are eager to see a big and fast ROI are the ones who become most vulnerable, a word more associated with femininity than masculinity. Not too long ago, I had a call from a guy who wanted to invest in an exotic fruit farm (I know, men and their exotics, you're seeing a trend). Just by Googling, in less than a minute, I knew he was being scammed. The people who had pitched him the deal were working in a boiler room in Irvine, California, and I knew it was a boiler room type of company, because I'd literally driven by the place every day when I was living out there. But he "knew better than a young girl."

Then why are you calling me? I wanted to ask, but I bit my tongue. He said he was sure he'd get a 20-30 percent return over the next six months and that he was going to do more research and get right back to me.

It was a teak wood farm, not a fruit farm at all, and it would be twenty years before anyone would be getting a return on it.

Not surprisingly, he never called back. I reached out to him a week later, and guess what? He'd already sunk a huge chunk of money into the so-called exotic fruit farm.

That's just one example. I have plenty. If someone is overconfident and wants to believe he's right, if he doesn't want to listen to a woman give him very good advice, he's simply not going to listen, even if it means risking a large sum of money on a very iffy-sounding deal.

But I also don't want to leave the impression that under confidence is a great tool to bring to the investment table. Many women are underconfident because they're new to investing and/or haven't been treated with respect by male advisors. Those women may do better than someone who trades too frequently, but they won't do as well as someone with a great financial professional helping her build her confidence and manage her money intelligently. Working with the right person or team to guide you on how to manage your money helps you develop the confidence you need to become a successful long-term investor, and for a woman, that person is probably another woman. She's been in your shoes, and she gets it. She has good information and advice, and you're ready to listen.

It's All in A Name: Advisor v. Planner

Terms can be confusing. I've had more than one new client ask me what the difference between a financial advisor and a financial planner is.

"Financial advisor" is a general term that includes subsets such as stockbrokers, insurance agents, money managers, estate planners, bankers, financial planners, and more. A financial planner is a professional who helps individuals and organizations create strategies to meet long-term financial goals. They're essential when you're establishing your master plan. *How will I set money aside for my children's educational costs? What should my goals be for retirement? How can I best structure my investments in relation to my taxes, and the like?* The planner will take a holistic approach, addressing budgeting, saving, investing, taxes, and retirement planning. Although many financial planners assist individual clients through their own practices, they might also work for a bank, wealth management firm, or nonprofit organization.

Financial planners usually hold licenses and/or designations like Certified Financial Planner (CFP), Chartered Financial Analyst (CFA), Chartered Financial Consultant (ChFC), or Certified Investment Management Analyst (CIMA), among others. The planner might have a specialty in investments, taxes, retirement, and/or estate planning. To obtain each of these licensures, the financial planner must complete a different set of education, examination, and work history requirements. A financial planner is a specific type of financial advisor.

"Financial advisor" is the general term for anyone who helps people manage their money. For a fee ranging from a couple hundred dollars per hour to thousands per year, your advisor assists with any number of money-related tasks. For example, a financial advisor might help manage investments, broker the sale and purchase of stocks and funds, or create a comprehensive estate and tax plan. They may operate much like a financial planner, even if they're not certified as one. Many work with finance and insurance companies, including securities and commodity brokers, banks, insurance carriers, and financial investment firms. However, many personal financial advisors are self-employed and operate small investment advisory firms.

Any advisor working with the public must hold a Financial Industry Regulatory Authority (FINRA) Series 65 license. Although the FINRA Series 65 licensing exam covers laws, regulations, ethics, and various topics important to the role of a financial advisor, candidates pass with as low a score as 72.5 percent. It's a broad exam that qualifies a person to claim proficiency in a wide variety of discrete and highly complex areas. Passing the exam doesn't prove much about expertise in any one area.

I am often known to say to someone who is puzzled about financial advisors, "Your advisor is not your friend. They don't care about you. Sorry." By that, I mean, of course, that they don't care about you *first.*

Financial advisors who work with large companies—including the Charles Schwab and Edward Jones of the world—have a responsibility first to that company, not to you. They're paid on commission and will not benefit purely because your investments are doing well. They're just cogs in a larger wheel, and they will generally advise you to put your money in one of the three funds they presented to the last client they talked to, help you choose one depending on your risk tolerance, and move on.

Or they'll try to sell you on their company's particular product, like life insurance or annuities. They may even be paid to sell you some other product. Most often, they don't have time to get to know you personally, especially if you're a woman without a huge fortune. Financial advisors, no matter what their backgrounds, will prioritize their time serving the clients with the largest accounts, and they'll stereotypically assume you're not one of them. Once again, you're back to not being taken seriously. "Don't pitch the bitch" gets translated in this forum as "don't pay attention to the female client." The financial industry is, after all, still a male-dominated culture. It's also possible with many financial advisors that they're not all that interested in your current investments because they're really after your will and trust—their firm makes real money on estate settlements.

I've met great financial advisors and lousy financial advisors. In the second category, two that stand out had careers that did not prepare them to serve clients well in this sector. One had just hung up his used car salesman's hat, and another his Lowe's apron. Not that there's anything wrong with working at a hardware store, but there's a big difference between knowing how to help someone buy the right supplies for her DIY garden project and having the skills to help someone grow their money. As for the used car salesman, that speaks for itself.

One last *caveat emptor*: Some independent advisors may not use a third-party custodian like a bank, brokerage firm, or similar institution. Your advisor is not necessarily a fiduciary. Bernie Madoff was a financial advisor. Can you say, "Ponzi scheme"?

Ms. Roboto

So, you don't want to waste money and time on a financial advisor, and you're just starting out as an investor. Maybe you have even already invested in a home, you're putting money into your 401k, and your salary has increased to the point where you have some discretionary income. However, you are far from having the assets necessary to be an accredited investor—a person with assets of at least $1 million (and that does not include your primary home). You've never invested before. What are your better options?

You are a great candidate for trying a robo-advisor, or "robo." Yes, the term sounds macho, but don't let that bother you. A robo is not a Schwarzenegger look-alike or a new version of C-3PO nattering around your kitchen. It's a digital platform that makes small investors' lives easier in the Twenty-First Century.

It's also a rather pathetic statement about my industry that I'm suggesting a robot can take better care of you than an actual living, breathing human being will. I'm a people person, so I'd much rather skip the self-checkout at Wegmans or Walgreens and instead go through the checkout where I can greet the clerk and have a friendly conversation. Maybe that describes you, too. But that clerk isn't charging me extra. It may also sound to you like it's a device that steals jobs from actual human beings, but that's not really true either. In today's digital world, most investing is done based on algorithms.

A robo-advisor at any firm, or primarily a robo-firm, provides algorithm-driven financial planning tailored to the customer via an app. You never have to wonder if a robo is recommending products that pad their bottom line, even when they're not the best products for you. A robo can't have a conflict of interest because if you don't do well, the firm doesn't do well. A robo won't tell clients what they want to hear, even if it's bad advice, just to keep them coming back. A robo doesn't want your money because they're hoping to settle your estate. A robo will always have a third-party custodian (a bank, brokerage firm, or similar entity), so your investments will be FDIC insured. (For whatever that's worth lol)

Although they require minimal human input, the best robos offer easy account setup, robust goal planning, account services, and portfolio management. Additionally, they offer security features, attentive customer service, comprehensive education, and, at the risk of sounding like a radio ad from the '50s, *low, low fees*. Yes, even lower than the 1 percent you'd be charged at Vanguard or Fidelity (although they too now offer robos with low, low fees).

One example of a financial tech ("fintech") firm known primarily for its robos, Ellevest, offers investing and wealth management online and through an app. And interestingly, Ellevest was founded by women to serve women.

CEO Sallie Krawcheck spent decades in financial services before founding Ellevest. She led Merrill Lynch Wealth Management and Smith Barney and was CFO, then CEO of Citigroup. She shares that one morning she had an "aha" moment that "stopped me in my tracks mid-mascara application." I can picture it, can't you? Staring at herself in the mirror, after years of being discounted by the men at the companies she now *led,* she pondered how the investing industry had been built and was primarily run by men, which means it was built *for* men. At that moment, she decided to make it her life's mission, as she says, "to unleash women's financial power and help them take control of their financial futures." Krawcheck moved quickly, carefully selecting a co-founder who would complement her skill set. Together with Charlie Kroll, they built a diverse team and established a service that even the most risk-averse, hesitant woman investor with limited funds would find welcoming and simple. Minimums? Nope. Quick, personal customer service even if you have just pennies in your account? Yep.

I share the Ellevest "herstory" because I identify with Krawcheck's mascara moment. I, too, experienced an "aha" when I realized the industry wasn't serving women. Only my moment had nothing to do with mascara.

I was at home in the middle of a birthday party when my new employer called to let me know that my services would no longer be needed. He was the employer who had hired me for my oil and gas expertise, who had presented themselves as a family-run, pro-woman business, and who didn't really want to hear my advice.

I ended that call and knew it was time.

To be honest, at that second, I was having more than a little of an F-you moment. I'd had enough of being told not to question things when I knew they needed to be rethought.

The very next day, I filed for an LLC and started the necessary paperwork to register a fund with the SEC. That was two-and-a-half-years ago, and in that time, I've raised more than $16.5 million (and counting) for that fund.

The family I was privileged to grow up in wasn't "exotic-fish-tank rich," but we were comfortable, especially up until the time my parents divorced. My parents were both financially savvy, and I was always encouraged to seize control of my financial future and employ entrepreneurial skills. My mother had her own financial advisor, a woman who has become a friend of the family and was very supportive to my mother when her life turned upside down through the divorce. At that point, my mother went back into the workforce and was flipping apartment buildings. She did—and continues to—a lot of reading and following the news, and sometimes makes even savvier investment choices than her advisor, who isn't afraid to compliment her when she does. I am aware that my background has enabled me to navigate complex systems more easily than others. I also had to put myself through college and learn how to manage my own limited funds, and I'm not afraid of making decisions, because I had to. All of these experiences taught and convinced me that creating generational wealth should not have been limited to the already wealthy. Through smart money decisions, targeted investing, and realistic planning, anyone can achieve financial freedom. Making the complex financial world accessible, particularly to those who have been excluded from it, is exactly what drives everything I do today.

Like Krawcheck, I'm in this business primarily (although not exclusively) for women. At Ellevest, men can also be clients, but the firm specializes in what is known as "gender-based" investing. That means their algorithms factor in women's generally lower incomes, earnings curves that differ from those of their male peers, and longer expected lifespans. They provide free educational programming that helps clients learn about everything from budgeting to retirement planning and low-priced memberships that include discounts for already affordable one-on-one coaching. They even offer career counseling that is gender-specific, including topics such as how to negotiate for a raise—a challenging task for women, no matter how good they are at "leaning in." Another perk is the ability to choose ethical investments based on your personal and political beliefs. For a woman new to investing and/or retirement planning with minimal funds, this kind of service is a powerful way to get started. And gender-based investing is something I keep at the forefront of my mind. The needs of women investors have been ignored for too long

According to NerdWallet, other top-rated robo's (not specifically geared to women) include SoFi, with no minimum or management fees, plus, free career counseling and "access" to CFPs; WealthFront, with a $500 minimum and a 0.25 percent management fee (after the first $5,000, on which there is zero management fee); and Marcus, by Goldman Sachs, with a $1,000 minimum and a 0.35 percent "advisory" fee. Some of these options also allow you to choose "value-based" investments. You don't have to do much research to determine which one is best for you.

I can't stress it enough. Robos are a great place to start.

Moving on. You've put some money aside, you have your "four-month rule" liquidity (the amount of cash you should keep handy in case of emergencies like a job loss or health crisis), and you are ready to embark on the next level of investing. Are there any good options for women out there who want to be taken seriously and not referred to as "the little lady?"

In all my time in sales, where I have been since I was fifteen years old, I've found it easier to work with female clients. I'd much rather pitch the bitch.

CHAPTER TWO

Is Patience A Virtue That Pays?

Everyone knows the old adage, "Patience is a virtue." And women are more virtuous in every way, right? Or at least socially and culturally expected—if not directly instructed—to be. So, of course, they're more patient than men.

Or are they?

The Old Testament of the Bible doesn't go into whether women are more patient investors or why, but it does present examples of saintly patience. Take, for example, Hannah.

In Western culture, there is no more powerful book than the Bible (Stay with me, I promise it makes sense), and in her story, as in many others, the notions of faithfulness and patience are intertwined. If you are wishing for something you still haven't received, the stories teach, then it just hasn't been the right time for you. *Be patient.* God will provide when the time is right.

Think, for example, about the old way of starting a family. In the early half of the Twentieth Century and before, if a wife didn't become pregnant, she didn't have the options we have today. If she were religious, she would pray to conceive.

I'm not suggesting that praying hurts if you want to make the most of your money, but it certainly isn't the only thing I'd recommend you do. While we're on cultural adages, "God helps those who help themselves."

While searching online for a summary of Hannah's story to refresh my Catholic girl memory of its bare bones, I went down a Bible study rabbit hole. On one website enumerating how characters from the Bible are models of good behavior in contemporary times, I came across an article published in 2018 entitled "*Heroic Women Of The Bible: Hannah — A Woman of Patience and Character*" by Kelly Wise Valdes.[7] The article itself is an example, not of a way of living I would recommend, but of folklore just as dangerous as fairy tales are when they're taken literally. I don't recommend waiting to be awakened by a prince to be swept into good fortune or sweeping hearths and daydreaming about palace balls. I know, what a surprise. These stories never really served women. They worked to uphold the patriarchy then, and they continue to do so now. That kind of behavior negatively affects women, teaching them passivity, a.k.a. accepting what you're given and forgoing what you're not. Such thinking prevents us women from taking charge of our futures.

Hannah appears in the Book of Samuel as a young married woman who is unable to have children. According to Valdes's interpretation, "It

7 Valdes, Kelly Wise, "Heroic Women Of The Bible — Hannah, A Woman Of Patience And Character," *The Osprey Observer,* January 26, 2018. https://www.ospreyobserver.com/2018/01/heroic-women-of-the-bible-hannah-a-woman-of-patience-and-character/. Accessed April 30, 2022.

is speculated that because Hannah was unable to have children, [her husband] Elkanah took another wife at Hannah's request." Of course, at the time, that wasn't out of the ordinary, but it's a piece of evidence that the lesson of Hannah's life might need to be updated—just a bit. Even though Elkanah's second wife, Peninnah, gave birth to several sons and a daughter, Elkanah was still more in love with Hannah. Valdes writes, "This caused substantial grief for both women. One wife was barren and wanted children and one wife fertile and wanted love."

What a scenario. It reminds me of the celebrity love triangles we see in tabloids and on social media: two women, one guy; only one person is happy, and it's not either woman. Remember Brad Pitt and Jennifer Aniston and how they couldn't get pregnant? Enter Angelina Jolie?

Okay, back to Hannah.

Apparently, instead of supporting one another, the two women simply couldn't get along—I know, *what a surprise.* Says Valdes, "Peninnah's jealousy caused her to torment Hannah, constantly mocking Hannah's inability to become pregnant. However, Hannah demonstrated grace and dignity by holding her tongue and continued to pray for a child." It seriously puts the film *Mean Girls* to shame.

This went on for *years.* Finally, one day as Hannah was silently mouthing her prayers at the temple, a priest named Eli asked her about her sorrows, and she promised God that if she had a son, she would "dedicate him to the priest." That did the trick. "God honored her diligence and patience," this current-day blogger goes on, "and Hannah gave birth to a son, Samuel. She kept him until he was weaned at about three years old. When the time came, she took him to the temple, just as she had promised, and dedicated him to God's service in a special ceremony." Even after finally getting her fondest wish, this poor woman had to hand her child over. No judgment of Valdes's personal beliefs, but the final lines of her retelling of this Bible story strike me as somewhat comical. She writes that Hannah "was blessed with more children: three sons and two daughters" and that "*The Bible bears no more mention of Peninnah.*"

Moral of the story: If we put our faith in God, we shall be rewarded.

Honestly? My personal faith is aligned with part of this lesson, i.e., a faith in a power greater than ourselves keeps us right-sized, grateful, and humble. I make a habit of expressing my gratitude to those who have helped me along the way and remembering to pay it forward.

These days, we can be proactive about many things. Thriving financially is one of them. It's really not a place to adhere to in *all of God's time.* I'm no Greek or Latin scholar, but I'm a lot fonder of the phrase *carpe diem.*

Risky Business

Over the years of my professional life, I have seen plenty of evidence that female clients are comfortable taking more time to make important money decisions, and naturally, I began to conclude that it was patience that explained their relative success as investors. However, there is no sound research to back up that impression. In fact, study after study proves me dead wrong. Talk about humility.

First of all, we're *all* less patient than in the past. Results of a survey of 3,000 Brits show patience is "becoming an exceedingly rare quality in modern society." According to the researchers, the subjects of the survey blamed gadgets and technology such as smartphones and on-demand TV. If you're on the receiving end of impatience, you know how uncomfortable it can be. But in the UK, even electrical appliances are bearing the brunt of

Twenty-First Century ants-in-the-pants. "Even a cup of tea, an undeniable symbol of British leisure time, incited anger among respondents if the kettle took more than 28 seconds to boil." According to the study, among the top twenty things that cause us to "lose our cool" are slow internet, delayed trains, waiting for the check in a restaurant, and even bad spelling. Most telling for our purposes, however, is Number 7: *People not listening.*[8]

Waiting for a return on investment did not make the list.

This relatively small sample showed women to be a tad more patient than men. Not so a survey of 80,000 people in seventy-six countries that showed women are actually *less patient* than their male peers by a small but significant margin, and that they are more risk averse.[9] Another study published the following year by a completely different team of researchers reinforces those outcomes and takes a closer look at other factors that make individuals risk averse.[10]

If you're in your mid-life, you'll be interested to know that researchers Daniel Horn and Hubert Janos Kiss found that middle-aged people have more patience than both younger and older people, with the elderly being significantly more risk-averse than the young. If you consider yourself one

8 Philippa Naylor, "Women are more patient than men, but both only last an average of two-and-a-half minutes," myhermes.co.uk, July 2011. https://pressreleases.responsesource.com/news/66034/women-are-more-patient-than-men-but-both-only-last/. Accessed May 17, 2022.

9 Falk, Armin, Anke Becker, Thomas Dohmen, Benjamin Enke, David Huffman, and Uwe Sunde, " Global Evidence on Economic Preferences," *The Quarterly Journal of Economics,* May 30, 2018. https://academic.oup.com/qje/article/133/4/1645/5025666. Accessed May 6, 2022.

10 Hórn, Daniel, and Hubert János Kiss, "Gender difference in risk aversion and patience: evidence from a representative survey," *SSRN Electronic Journal,* January 2019. https://www.researchgate.net/publication/330414556_Gender_differences_in_risk_aversion_and_patience_evidence_from_a_representative_survey. Accessed May 2, 2022.

of the sharper tools in the shed, you may also be more patient. In the US, higher cognitive ability accompanies greater patience (there's no established causation, only correlation). If you have two or more kids and have had to master yogic breathing to avoid going ballistic on a regular basis, you'll be fascinated to read this one. One study, conducted with women and men in rural India, showed more patience in their female subjects than in their male peers, and that *women with a greater number of children exhibit more patience than women with fewer* [emphasis mine].[11] Interestingly, researchers extrapolated from their analysis that the more women are willing to wait, the less likely they are to make good decisions regarding the future of the family.[12] Those conclusions support my instinctive belief that preaching to women that patience alone is what makes women investors more successful is not only counter-intuitive but just flat-out wrong.

So, if blind patience and faith like Hannah's in the Bible aren't what are driving the strong performance of women investors, what is?

All three of the above studies discussed risk aversion in detail, which, of course, is a determining factor in investing. My theory is that what can be misperceived as women's general patience is actually a combination of caution, realism, and under confidence—the latter likely caused by the fact that Boston Consulting Group found that 73 percent of female investors feel so underestimated by their advisors that they're eager to switch.[13] In addition,

---

11 Bauer, Michal, and Julie Chytilová, *IZA,* June 2009. https://ftp.iza.org/dp4241.pdf. Accessed April 24, 2022.
12 Ibid.
13 Paradi, Judy, and Paulette Filion, "Why women leave their financial advisors and how to prevent it," *StrategyMarketing.ca,* p.6. https://www.strategymarketing.ca/wp-content/uploads/Why-women-leave-their-financial-advisors-and-how-to-prevent-it.pdf. Accessed May 10, 2022.

- Women tend to be more focused on long-term security and safety than a quick return on investment (ROI).
- Women live longer, on average, than men, which explains why they're looking at the long-term.
- Women say that security is one of their top priorities.
- Women are willing to listen to experts and their interpretations of data and research.
- Women have less to invest overall due to the gender pay gap and are thus more careful with what they do have.

I've seen all of the above, as the below case studies show.[14]

First Gen Wealth

One of our good friends, Stephen, is an orthopedic surgeon, and his wife is a stay-at-home mom whose working on an accounting degree (yay!). I've been inviting Stephen to networking events and conferences in an attempt to make him aware he should give his finances some real thought. Recently, he said, "These events make me realize I don't know anything else... All I know are bones. All I learned was medicine."

It's not unusual for specialists in any field to feel that way.

In most cases, doctors end up in investment groups but have no idea what's really going on. When a physician comes to me, it's because they've had a moment of awakening, "Oh, maybe I should understand what's going on with my money!"

14 I've changed my clients' names to protect their privacy.

I'm working with an anesthesiologist who is getting to the point where she's eager to work a bit less. Obviously, the pandemic has led to a lot of healthcare professionals being burned out. She doesn't want to check out entirely because she's dedicated to helping people. Even though she started her career late in life, after the military, she's been able to build up enough wealth to start investing. Someone told her to talk to a CFA if she was really interested in retiring, and the advisor told her she wasn't at all set up to retire. She panicked.

When she came to me, I reassured her, sharing that I'm not a big fan of financial advisors (and that's euphemistic). I advised her to take everything they say with a grain of salt, and that they wouldn't want her to move her money because it's a pain in their … neck, so they'd probably make it as difficult as possible. But moving her money was in her best interest.

People without time to even think about it—and how would an anesthesiologist really have time to focus on money, over the past few years in particular, considering the demands on them—are unaware that large companies, including financial advisors like Edward Jones, are basically engaged in stealing your money. In fact, places like Edward Jones are the first in line. They have their fingers in it.

She sent an email to her advisor asking them to close her accounts so she could move them over to a different custodian. These were people who had been managing her accounts forever. Then she went out of town on a much-needed two-week vacation. When she came back, her accounts had not been liquidated. They'd basically ignored her request, and it had cost her about 10 percent. She told me about it, and I urged her to call them and speak to them directly. That's what I mean—they will make it as difficult as possible. Imagine if she handled her professional life that way!

Physicians are an interesting group. Typically, they work a lot, and they spend a lot. The lifestyle is a certain way that leads them to maintain appearances among their peers, you know, like the large home and sports cars. For example, the partners in Stephen's practice are running around purchasing a lot of assets that have no long-term worth, their primary real estate aside. Thankfully, Stephen doesn't subscribe to that mindset. But, they will have to really dig into their finances to figure out what to do with all their income, but neither he nor his wife have any experience being in that position.

One example of how doctors are totally out of the loop with the financial industry. Stephen asked me if he could borrow money through me in order to buy into his practice. I am not the person you want to borrow money from; I take a high percentage. I told him to try his bank, which of course went super smoothly due to the income coming in through the practice. If a bank didn't lend to someone like him, they probably shouldn't be a bank. But the point is, specialists have been hyper-focused on their fields. They haven't had time to learn what other people do.

My client Jamie is another great example. She's only thirty-two years old, but recently received an impressive bonus from the personal injury law firm where she works. Her boyfriend, Adam, talked up crypto-currencies and non-fungible assets (known as NFTs), and pointed her to a couple of websites. She told me that she cruised the internet for "way too many hours" and still didn't understand any of it. We looked at the sites Adam had recommended. Jamie told me that Adam had said, "They're totally legit. Everyone knows about them." But as a lawyer, she was trained to be suspicious, and her instincts were right. She'd been browsing the type of open marketplace sites where investors buy digital art—the absolute worst way to invest in NFT.

Adam, who grew up with money, loved to play the market in all different kinds of ways. But Jamie shared that she'd been part of a legal team that won a huge lawsuit with a settlement unlike anything she would see again for a while, if ever. She didn't think about her cash as "Monopoly money," she said.

With the sum of money Jamie had to invest and her goal of long-term security, she was ready to investigate some alternatives with excellent ROIs that Adam had never even heard of. The last time she and I talked, she told me she'd taken the quiz on herfirst100k.com to determine her "investment personality." I let her talk. She told me she was super impressed with Tori Dunlap, who created the site, and asked me if I knew her.

I don't, I told her, and then guided her carefully through the site so she could see how Dunlap actually makes her money: marketing tools and apps that "help" women learn financial literacy and providing space for copy produced by firms seeking clients (what in the old days was called "advertorials"). There's absolutely nothing wrong with marketing other companies' products, especially when you're as upfront about it as Dunlap is. Frankly, it's impressive what Dunlap has done by finding a niche and filling a gap, but with my help, Jamie quickly figured out the difference between an investment professional and an influencer-slash-pundit in the tradition of Dave Ramsey. Dunlap actually pokes fun at the Dave Ramseys of the world, who make their money pushing all types of financial instruments for their sponsors. And I'm with her on that. I also appreciate the way she's drawn attention to the fact that women need more financial literacy.

But it's also important to understand the difference between what I do and what you'll find on a site loaded with affiliate links and sponsored content.

There are also those charlatans out there selling Twenty-First Century investment snake oil via conferences that supposedly turn you into a fund manager in three days (cough, cough, Bridger Pennington and his $695 conferences perennially discounted to $295 at www.InvestmentFundsSecrets.com). I've stumbled into those kinds of things in large hotels only to see a giant conference room stuffed with eager male faces—and maybe a few women who, I assume, didn't want to send their partners off unsupervised. Because surely we women are not so gullible as to believe we can become experts at *anything* in seventy-two hours. In addition to those types of "opportunities," there are plenty of seminars delivered by empowerment experts who count on you believing that once you are fired up, you'll hit pay dirt in the investment world.

I can't even.

Finally, there are the women who didn't grow up around money and find themselves single without ever having figured it out.

Judy came to me in her mid-forties. She'd recently been divorced and was re-establishing her once lucrative career after years outside the paid workforce. She shared that years before, she'd attended the first few financial planning meetings her husband had set up, but although she'd asked good questions (she had a business degree), they talked over her, often more interested in banter about their recent golf outings, where she figured the real discussions happened.

Eventually, Judy stopped attending the meetings and ended up entrusting her husband with long-term financial planning and investments. "After all," she said, "it felt like it was his money. Now, I know better.

And with my divorce settlement, I'm going to take my time and research everything. Now that I've seen the financials, it's obvious he did a good job but was way more risk tolerant than I am. Plus, I just plain disagree with some of his choices. Honestly, I think I could have done better on my own!"

She was probably right. One example was her husband's choice to invest in annuities (one of his golf buddies sold insurance products). He was soon frustrated by the low returns—about 2 percent per year. He moved the money five years in and paid a hefty penalty. (We didn't discuss if he still played golf with that guy.) Judy was extremely curious about alternative investments for both stability and higher returns. We quickly established a good relationship in which each of us listens attentively to the other.

Yes, there is a gender difference in investing.

At the risk of sounding reductive about the differences between men and women's approaches to investing, I see basic tendencies I can't ignore. For example, my female clients are inquisitive in a way that is not common with men, who apparently have a greater need to maintain the facade of a level of knowledge that they may not actually possess. Women are usually a bit less competitive, and thus, willing to admit they *need* or *would like* to do more research, listen to an expert, and think things through. Most do not suffer from the unfortunate cultural expectations our society places on men to avoid admitting feeling under confident or under prepared. Those expectations basically train men to behave like they are NFL coaches and quarterbacks after the game has been played.

There are exceptions to every rule. Of course, I occasionally have a male client who hasn't been cowed by Twenty-First Century American toxic masculinity, and naturally I also get the odd female client who is as much of a daredevil in investing as she may be on a rock-climbing adventure or ski slope. I've had female clients who were in too much of a rush and too eager to see a big ROI to listen to and appreciate my expertise. But in general, the case studies I've provided show the difference between female and male investors.

I pay close attention to their personalities, risk tolerance, goals, and histories and give women the respect we deserve, and—imagine that—they get super into the whole process and gain financial literacy while they make smart investment choices. Communication is key to our relationships, and that in itself makes women investing with women unique. For a woman who has just gone through a major life change, for example, having another woman at the table is comforting; the same holds true for someone new to the investing world.

Lest you think I'm alone in coming to these conclusions, I'm not. Other female investment advisors I know have opinions that go beyond what I've noticed, including such observations as "Women have more self-control." Could that be because they've been brought up to be restrained and patient? Another thing I've heard is "Women don't like to let go." That basically translates, in this realm, as seeing their money grow at a respectable rate and thus avoiding trading. Stocks or funds that are sold after less than a year are taxed at a short-term capital gains rate, which is typically higher than the long-term capital gains rate you'd pay if you held onto a stock or fund for more than a year before selling, so the effects of those decisions are immediate. Or a woman client can be holding too much cash, which my colleagues agree is a sign of fear—just another result of inexperience and a lack of good coaching, being talked down to, or steering completely clear to avoid uncomfortable situations with condescending male advisors such that their entire portfolio, should they have one, is in disarray. And my peers have also experienced the difficulty of working with male clients. One friend actually said to me, "Men think they don't need my advice."

It's something we've all noticed in our families. When women have problems, they tend to want to talk it out and receive support. Their husbands, fathers, brothers, and male friends—usually to their own detriment—hopscotch right over those needs and provide advice. Yet they rarely, if ever, ask for any. Some psychologists believe it's one of the reasons our divorce rate is so high.

The Investment Industrial Complex

If you aren't a fan of observations that are, like mine, pretty much anecdotal, no matter how certain I am about the trends I've observed firsthand, there are recent studies that scientifically identify that women investors do better working with women advisors. One longitudinal study from the UK found:

> Women with good advisors perceive themselves to have a higher risk tolerance than before and invest 10.6%--points more than self-directed investors ... [and] the investor-advisor gender combination matters, but only for female investors. Women with male advisors are more risk averse, feel less knowledgeable and less confident about their investment decisions. They also invest 11%--points less than women with female advisors. Indeed, female investors advised by women report the highest risk tolerance and make the lowest

> portfolio allocation to risk-free assets across the full sample, including men.[15]

The authors summarize by writing, "Having a male advisor appears particularly toxic" for a woman investor.

What didn't work for me as a female employee doesn't work for female clients. Maybe it's trite, but we women need one another.

But of course, it's not all due to essentialism—behaving in ways determined by the parts you were born with—any more than whether you prefer pants or a skirt, flats or heels, baseball or ballet, makeup or *au naturel.* It's socialization, expectations, reinforcement of historic gender roles, and a heavily patriarchal investment industrial complex that may hire women but doesn't want them making any big decisions. Ye Olde Boys' Club. They don't want to share what they have, and they don't want to share what they know.

That's the problem, right there. Women in finance have been universally ignored by the powers that be, whether they're clients, employees, or coworkers. Success in investing comes from expertise and education. In addition to new levels of risk tolerance for us impatient but investment-cautious two-legged called *women*, education and experience are what we lack and what we need. I know this to be true because of my own experience. Once we know what we are doing, we are unstoppable.

Astronaut John Glenn never would have made it into orbit and safely back to planet Earth without smart women. During the US-Soviet space race, NASA hired a group of African American female mathematicians

---

15 Baekström, Ylva, Ian W. Marsh, and Jo Silvester, "Financial Advice and Gender; Wealthy Individual Investors in the U.K.," August 13, 2021. https://papers.ssrn.com/sol3/papers.cfm?abstract_id=3286336. Accessed May 12, 2022.

who became, as IMDb states, "the brains behind one of the greatest operations in US history." Dorothy Vaughn, Mary Jackson, and Katherine Gobels Johnson rose through the ranks of NASA along with many other great thinkers and became known as "human computers." However, their real names and stories weren't widely known until the 2016 film "Hidden Figures," which told their life stories from whip-smart schoolgirls to true American heroes.

There has yet to be a film about women in finance. It's certainly not because we're doing something wrong. It may be because we haven't broken enough laws. And even so, we're outperforming the men.

We're the Investment Industrial Complex's best kept secret.

$

CHAPTER THREE

Understanding Women as Investors

> "You know how you just breathe in and fully expect air? You don't say to yourself, *oh, God — I hope there's enough air when I go for this next breath!* And when you go to the beach you're not worried they're going to run out of waves. You just *know.* It's there. You don't even think about it .... That's how you can be about money." – Terry McMillan, "How to Make a Lot of Money," *Women Talk Money,* 2022

Most women who read fiction know the name Terry McMillan, and it would be hard to find a Black woman, reader or otherwise, who doesn't. McMillan burst onto the publishing scene in 1992 and changed it forever with her bestselling "crossover" (read by both Black and white readers) novel *Waiting to Exhale.* Forest Whitaker directed the 1995 screen version with a star-studded cast including Angela Bassett and Whitney Houston, which took in $14 million the weekend it was released, rocketing it into first place at the box office.

But few people know that just a couple of years before that, McMillan met a financial consultant in Beverly Hills she calls "BHML": the Beverly Hills Money Lady. In the recently released book, *Women Talk Money*, edited by memoirist and feminist Rebecca Walker, McMillan tells the story of how that random incident changed her life. (Or was it random? It depends on your beliefs around synchronicity.) McMillan writes that she was in a period when she was "particularly scared about money."[16] And the unnamed woman, BHML, announced she considered it "her highest spiritual calling to help women know the truth about money."[17]

Amen to that. For me, meeting BHML would be like finding a sister of a different mother—to hell with the color of our skin.

But McMillan didn't respond as I would, or even as you might think, and neither do a lot of the women I talk to about their beliefs and assumptions around investing and creating a sound and/or spectacular financial future for themselves. McMillan writes, "Did I want to know the truth about money? Not really, tbh."[18] She goes on to explain that her primary belief about money, at the time was that it was hard to get, and even harder to hold onto.

Furthermore, other people can have money—they can have a lot of it, tons of it, really—and you know many of those people; they were your friends growing up, they're your friends now, and they're your son's friends, too, but you've never been one of those people, and you never will be. To summarize, the truth about money would go something like this: *There might be enough. (Just barely.) But there will never be a lot.*[19]

---

16 Rebecca Walker, ed., *Women Talk Money.* NY: Simon and Schuster, 2022, 283.
17 Walker, 283.
18 Walker, 283.
19 Walker, 283.

Sound anything like that critical voice in your head?

But McMillan changed it all up, and you can, too. Two decades later, McMillan writes she is astonished by how much money she has:

> [My grandchild] Little Tracy thinks I have a lot of money. Even Big Tracy is starting to think so. I go to Europe. Sleep on fancy sheets. Own my own small but lovely home. Paid cash for my kid's private liberal arts college. I even (this is almost embarrassing) fly first-class sometimes. I also have a will, an S corp, and some other white-man money thing called a Cash Balance Plan .... I don't say all this to brag. I say it because my mother was a prostitute, and my dad was a drug dealer and the fact that I just paid cash for my kid's private liberal arts college blows my fucking mind.[20]

And, dear reader, *that* tells you the real truth about money. It's there to be had, it's there to be invested in, and it's there to be grown if you know how to do it right—or have someone who will help you do that.

If you're thinking it sounds like a lot of woo-woo "I can manifest anything" thinking, hold on just a minute. It's easy to mock the *Law of Attraction*, considering you and I might suspect at first glance that it's no more productive to meditate on positive outcomes like followers of Esther and Jerry Hicks than to pray to God like Hannah in the Bible.[21] But in the midst of *The Law of Attraction* vortex of marketing and workshopping lies a truism: you won't have what you need if you don't put your mind to it. There is real wisdom in *paying attention* and *directing your focus.* Plus, taking the right steps and believing your efforts will pay off? Both are key. After all, no one's going to do it for you or believe in you if you don't. The

---

20 Walker, 284.
21

fact that you're reading this book? That shows you're already manifesting. And listening to BHML was perhaps Terry McMillan's first go at it.

Note: At least relying on the Law of Attraction and manifesting positive change doesn't mean you have to hand over your firstborn to the temple like Hannah had to. Furthermore, I didn't go to an expensive liberal arts college, and I'm doing just fine, thank you. But more on that another time. For now, let's turn to how Warren Buffet has done it, because there is an entire book written on how he does it, much like women do, and if I'm doing fine, he's doing … well ...

Eight of the Many Reasons Warren Buffett is a Legend

In *Warren Buffett Invests Like a Girl: And Why You Should, Too,* Louann Lofton lists eight similarities between Buffett's investing and the investing particular to women:

1. Trade less than men do.
2. Exhibit less overconfidence: men think they know more than they do, while women are more likely to know what they don't know.
3. Shun risk more than male investors do.
4. Be less optimistic and therefore more realistic than their male counterparts.
5. Put in more time and effort researching possible investments, considering every angle and detail, as well as considering alternate points of view.
6. Be more immune to peer pressure and tend to make decisions the same way regardless of who's watching.
7. Learn from their mistakes.

8. Have less testosterone than men do, making them less willing to take extreme risks, which, in turn, could lead to less extreme market cycles.[22]

We have covered #1—#4 in prior chapters. We've also touched on #5, how women research more than men do, but let's take a closer look at what that means.

Principle: If you don't get it, don't buy it.

If you were an investment consultant in the early part of the Twenty-First Century, you were likely dealing with a lot of confused clients. You may even have been confused yourself! But no matter how hard asset managers tried, there were still millions of people left scratching their heads about where they were putting their money. *High-yield mortgage-backed securities + derivatives = headache.* If you bought in, you were violating a very basic principle of investing: *Know what you own.*

If you haven't yourself experienced the "cocktail party stock-tip moment," you've probably seen it in films. The all-time most famous example is from the 1971 classic film *The Graduate,* when Mr. McGuire (Walter Brooke) leans in toward Benjamin (Dustin Hoffman) and says, "I just want to say one word to you. Just one word." Benjamin, who is focused less on ROI than on Mrs. Robinson, possibly the origin of the term MILF, replies, "Yes, sir." "Are you listening?" McGuire asks. "Yes, I am," replies the distracted Benjamin. And Mr. McGuire states that one word: "Plastics." Confused, his eyes darting, Benjamin asks, "Exactly how do you mean?"

22 Loann Lofton, *Warren Buffett Invests Like a Girl: And Why You Should, Too,* with a foreword by Tom Gardner. NY: HarperCollins, 2011, 44.

and McGuire replies, "There's a great future in plastics. Think about it. Will you think about it?"[23]

For many, it's an old friend of Dad's or a buddy from college who is working on Wall Street. But whoever it is who delivers that sort of line to you, designating some investment opportunity that is the next-best-thing-since-sliced-bread, take a deep breath. Maybe it is good advice. "Plastics" certainly was. Even though Benjamin might have guilt today about all those Dasani bottles polluting the ocean, he certainly would have made a fortune. But when you hear a tip like that—and if you never have, I assure you, you will—either thank the guy who by sharing feels savvy and superior or dodge him as fast as possible. If his tip or scheme interests you, make a mental note to do some research. That's what you'd do anyway, without my suggesting it. Right?

Think about how much research it takes to buy a house, a car, or even a new laptop or phone. But when people are investing in public companies, they're often just going on the word of someone whose recommendation sounded good. We have immense resources at our fingertips when researching; no longer do we have to dredge around in Moody's and Standard & Poor's reports like Buffett did when he was just starting out. We are both blessed and cursed with the internet. Blessed because it's all right there; cursed because it is so damn hard to tell what's biased and what's not. (That's where someone like me comes in handy.)

Just like you have to know what you're reading, you seriously need to know what you're buying, and studies show that women spend more time researching and seeking expert advice (and then taking it) than do men. In fact, I often wonder how many male audience members left the theater and

23 *The Graduate* 1967. https://www.imdb.com/title/tt0061722/characters/nm0111754

called their brokers, instructing them to buy plastic. (And how much they may have made on the ahead-of-the-times buy; Coke and Pepsi switched to plastic bottles in 1978, seven years after *The Graduate* came out.)

I needed to learn this lesson myself. When I was living in California, I spent a lot of time working with companies using capital I raised, advising them on how to adopt practices that would help them grow and be profitable, which in turn would help my clients. That took a lot of patience, as older businesspeople often looked at me as if I were a child. If I knew nothing about their companies, I couldn't contribute anything very meaningful. But I did. So, I could stipulate that the capital I was bringing was, for example, to hire an accountant or purchase some software that they sorely needed. But often, they'd do what they wanted to do with the capital anyway. I was left wondering why I was doing all that extra work, only to have to give disappointing news to investors. Or I'd get involved with some tech startup that was one of a million that might or might not work out—the odds aren't that different from getting into Harvard or winning the lottery. Again, I would be dealing with something over which I had no control, and it was totally possible they'd use the capital I was able to bring them for something not very well thought out.

Even Warren Buffett, despite being heavily invested in giants like Amazon, Microsoft, and Apple, doesn't feel comfortable trying to predict the future cash flows of smaller tech companies because the field is so fast-moving and constantly changing. Nothing, after all, is future proof, and that's an understatement in tech. Stepping back to trait #2 for a moment, Buffett is willing to admit what he doesn't know. I had to become just as willing.

In 2018, I moved back to Texas, where I could raise capital for companies I grew up working for, companies that I understand, and are run by people I know. Which brings up another lesson to be learned from Buffett: it's easy to forget that research doesn't begin and end with annual reports and the internet. Buffett doesn't only want to know a*bout* the C-suite; he wants to *know* the C-suite. Editor and cofounder of The Corporate Library Neil Minow once said, "I think one of the most impressive things about [Buffett] is not the way he looks at stocks, although gosh knows he is very good at math, but the way he looks at people."[24] When I returned home to Texas, I was able to re-establish relationships, and relationships are invaluable in this industry.

Let's take oil and gas, a good place to put money, despite global instabilities like war and the environmental toll. These companies are growing in value, but many people are concerned about the long-term prospects, for obvious reasons. But I know which companies are honestly working toward transitions to green energy, not just green-washing. Having learned from the tech industry, I'm very attentive to a company's future proofing! And, like most women, I'm interested in supporting companies that are doing the right thing not only for their employees, clients, and/or customers, but also for the planet.

> Buffett continues to hold to a statement he made in 1986 in his Shareholder Letter:
>
> We intend to continue our practice of working only with people we like and admire. This policy not only maximizes our chances for good results, but it also ensures us an extraordinarily good time. On the other hand,

24 Neil Minow, interview with Chris Hill of The Motley Fool, September 22, 2010.

> working with people who cause your stomach to churn seems much like marrying for money—probably a bad idea under any circumstances, but absolute madness if you are already rich.[25]

Truer words were never spoken. Especially in these days of "Black Lives Matter" and "#MeToo," it's pretty easy to determine where the good guys and the not-so-good guys are. The women investors I work with want to know those details, and they pay close attention to them—as do I.

Louann Lofton, author of the aforementioned 2011 book, *Warren Buffett Thinks Like a Girl,* stresses that this strategy—knowing what you're investing in and understanding it—is as important as many others Buffett has relied on to become the legend he is:

- Benefiting from "float," or using cash that has been paid to an insurance company, for example, and is available until a claim must be covered.

- Investing only in companies that have wide "moats," or a safe differential between the stock price today and the true value.

- Avoiding overconfidence.

In fact, how do you know the value of a company if you don't understand it? Lofton introduces the notion of a "circle of competence," or the area in which you are well-versed. After listing a number of large companies

---

25 Warren E. Buffett, Berkshire Hathaway 1986 Shareholder Letter, in Buffett and Lawrence A. Cunningham, *The Essays of Warren Buffett,* 2nd ed., Durham, NC: Carolina Academic Press, 50.

in which Buffett has invested over the years—including Coca-Cola, Nike, Procter & Gamble, and others—she points out that "investing [is] relatable when you can look around and see the evidence of your money at work." She gives as an example Oreos, from Kraft Foods, but it works as well with Crest at the CVS or Nike running shoes at the mall. Plus, knowing what the company you're investing in does makes the adventure more enjoyable. As Lofton says, "It's just not as jazzy to say, 'Hey, I own the company that applies the coating of the oxide layers onto the aluminum electrolytic capacitors of this very computer's motherboard!'"[26]

Of course, if you're an expert in something as esoteric as the elements of the systems necessary to bring oil and gas into homes and commercial properties, as I happen to be, or in pharmaceuticals, as you might be, then go for it. But also look at the "moat" and be sure it's wide; and also look at the people running the castle and make sure they're upstanding. The point is, buy what you know, and don't forget to pay special attention to the people running the show. We women are models at that.

Additional dangers of testosterone

Lofton also stresses the importance of two more elements of Buffett's strategy: "Be honest with yourself and remember the perils of overconfidence"[27]—usually not a problem for women investors—and focus on the "positives of pessimism." Quoting Buffett himself, she writes, "'When investing, pessimism is your friend, euphoria the enemy.'"[28] And both of these tips are related to avoiding confirmation bias and remaining realistic.

---

26 Lofton, 63.
27 Lofton, 63.
28 Lofton, 73.

What do I mean by "confirmation bias"? We all understand it these days thanks to the algorithms that construct our social media feeds. Meta, the parent company of Facebook, developed this tool to increase the number of hits on a page, which in turn enables them to charge more for advertising. In 2007, Facebook introduced the "Like" button, helping them understand what users enjoy seeing in their feeds. That was the beginning. Soon after, they implemented EdgeRank, the algorithm that for years determined what news would appear in your feed along with photos of your niece. Since 2018, Facebook's most recent algorithm relies on more than 100,000 factors to determine who and what appears in your feed. So, if you tended to like posts about Bernie Sanders back in 2016, you'd receive posts from *The Washington Examiner* about Hillary Clinton running a sex-trafficking ring out of a pizza parlor in D.C. In 2022, if you enjoy reading conspiracy theories stating that Rothschild and other companies led by Jewish people are sending space lasers to earth to ignite California wildfires, you'll see posts about US Rep. Marjorie Taylor Greene's (R-GA) campaign.[29] When it comes to investing, if you are a member of Extinction Rebellion or another climate change activism organization, you may see articles from *The Intercept* about Exxon's history of lying to the public about the dangers of spewing too much carbon into the atmosphere; if you invest in oil and gas companies, you may see *Wall Street Journal* posts about fuel companies that are transitioning to green energy. None of these news articles alone are a good basis for investing. We all tend to believe what we read when we approve of the (usually biased) source. Men, more than women, are

29 Zach Beauchamp, "Marjorie Taylor Greene's Space Laser and the Age-Old Problem of Blaming the Jews," *Vox*, January 30, 2021. Accessed May 9, 2022. https://www.vox.com/22256258/marjorie-taylor-greene-jewish-space-laser-anti-semitism-conspiracy-theories

inclined to believe what they believe is right and are reluctant to entertain other perspectives.

Forgive me for momentarily digressing to include here one of the best "Bushisms" ever. In July 2021, fellow Texan and former President George W. Bush unfortunately said, "I know what I believe. I will continue to articulate what I believe and what I believe—I believe what I believe is right."

Most men, in their infinite need to maintain confidence, also have more trouble than women do admitting that they've made a mistake, and if you can't admit you've made one, you can't learn from it. Warren Buffett breaks down his mistakes much the way Catholics do sins—omission and commission—and he has no trouble confessing them. In the first case, he's referring to an opportunity missed; in the second, to something he did that he lived to regret (even if learning from it lessens the remorse). He claims that missed opportunities, like failing to buy into Wal-Mart in the 1990s at a particularly low price, bother him more than the active choices he's made that later he wishes he hadn't. I get that. Sometimes, if you make a choice and work diligently to turn it profitable only to fail, at least you tried. Buffett experienced that early in his career, acquiring Berkshire Hathaway in 1962, when it was a large textile enterprise. That business was fated to fail, but in the 1980s he salvaged the company name and used it as an umbrella under which to buy insurance companies and use the float to invest. He achieved a masterful transformation of the company despite the eventual loss of the manufacturing division.

All you can do is acknowledge the misstep, study what went wrong, and analyze it. It's good material with a lot of teaching power. Even Buffett has made some big ones, including purchasing Berkshire Hathaway in the belief he could save its textile manufacturing. And then there was the epic failure of his investment in US Airways (US Air until 1996), when he played the part of the "white knight" to protect the company from a corporate raider. Later, he said that his analysis of the company had been superficial and that he should have seen that a lack of government regulation would lead the industry to eat itself alive. He was able to cash out without a loss but breaking even is not the goal; it meant his capital was tied up in US Airways when it could have been getting a good return elsewhere. Interestingly, considering our topic, Lofton reports that Buffett once said, "'If only women could be CEOs of companies that flew planes I think it would be a lot better,' and concluded that testosterone is responsible for 'air-aholism.'"[30]

What provides an excellent segue into the last reason women are better than men at investing: less testosterone.

A 2006 study of the returns on all US mutual funds and the different results between those managed by men and those managed by women showed that women had less extreme investment styles and that their persistence led to more consistent returns. The graph of their earnings showed no dramatic spikes or bottoms, and that in itself is a worthy goal for a fund manager like me. Add to that the evidence that female-managed hedge funds returned, in the first decade of this century, an average of 9.06 percent versus the 5.82 percent weighted average of other hedge funds. During the market panic of 2008, women-managed funds suffered about 10 percent losses, compared to the other funds' nearly 20 percent.[31]

One of the most interesting aspects of this line of analysis is that the market itself is safer when it's not run by men. Like any business,

30 Lofton, 23.
31 Lofton, 24-25.

diversification would lead to stability. If you haven't yet seen the classic 1983 Wall Street comedy "Trading Places," it's time. I guarantee Dan Akroyd and Eddie Murphy will make you laugh so hard your face will hurt. But on top of that, it has a practically prototypical scene from the commodities floor as one scheme to make a killing on orange juice futures plays out. Without spoilers, basically, some shenanigans with crop reports and projections lead to frenzy, and the aggressive behavior as brokers compete for the kill are illustrative. If you think shopping at Harrod's of London's annual sale is dangerous, you've never been on the market floor.

> A 2008 study from the University of California, Santa Barbara, found:
>
> [W]hen men are being observed and judged by other men; they tend to make riskier decisions than necessary … in an attempt to assert dominance. Worse still, even when the outcome would have been exactly the same had less risk been taken, the guys *still* chose the riskier path.[32]

If there had been more women involved in the financial industry in the years prior to 2008, perhaps there would have been less instability and the number of financially devastated Americans would have been significantly lower. Not only do women perform better as investors, but their presence in the financial world as consultants, brokers, and investors would make America perform better.

I am woman, hear me roar

I do not mean to suggest, however, that women do not engage in competition among peers. Even in the examples taken from *Women Talk*

32 Lofton, 27.

Money, we see the "humble brag" from women who never thought they'd have any money: both Terry McMillan and Rebecca Walker boast that they were able to put their kids through college. As far as I'm concerned, they deserve more than a humble brag. How about a little swagger, ladies?

In my experience, women also take a lot of pleasure in being some of the biggest donors in the room, be it at a school auction or as a billionaire philanthropist (#MacKenzieScott). But that's a different type of competition, and one that can lead to positive outcomes, not a scramble and chaos on the stock market floor and volatility that affects millions of Americans.

If you're going to show off, competing with your peers, what better time to do so than *after* you have actually reaped outstanding excellent ROI? I have absolutely nothing against that, and I just might occasionally do it myself.

> We must trust our own thinking.
>
> Trust where we are going.
>
> And get the job done.
>
> — Wilma Mankiller

Wilma Pearl Mankiller was a Native American (Cherokee Nation) activist and social worker. Her last name, Mankiller, stems from her being the first woman elected to serve as Principal Chief of the Cherokee Nation. It signifies accomplishment and honor, not psychopathy. And her words, above, apply so perfectly to what I am hoping readers of this book will embrace. We women *are* the best investors out there. We need to trust ourselves and take action.

In *What's Your Story? A Journal for Everyday Evolution,* Rebecca Walker and Lily Diamond write that it is time for us to examine the assumptions and expectations we carry into our lives.

> These are ideas you've learned about the way you are, the way other people are, and the way the world is and should be. These ideas are passed down from family, parents, and caregivers; they're taken on from friends and colleagues, and they're impressed upon you by any number of sociopolitical, religious, and cultural systems of belief.
>
> For example, for many centuries, scientists maintained that people with different skin colors were genetically distinct and categorized them into five "races." Yet there is far more genetic variation in people with the same skin color than there is between those with different skin colors. The truth tells a different story about who we are … [33]

The truth challenges the ideologies that white people have used to repress Black people for generations upon generations. The truth challenges the way that (mostly white) men have been regarded as better investors than women, whether they are white, BIPOC, cis, or LGBTQ+.

After meeting BHML, Terry McMillan faced the real truth about money: it's there to be had and it's there to be grown. She went out there and proved those white guys wrong. I am here to tell you that can you too.

33 Rebecca Walker and Lily Diamond, *What's Your Story? A Journal for Everyday Evolution,* Boulder, CO: Sounds True, 2020, 17.

Chapter 4

The Power of Wealth

"*Women with money and women with power are two uncomfortable ideas in our society.*" — Candace Bushnell

If you've ever watched ABC's hit show "Shark Tank," you know who Lori Greiner and Barbara Corcoran are. These are two women who, unlike the profile of the conservative female investor we've been describing for several chapters, spend their days encouraging and supporting others to take risks. In fact, it was their own risk-taking that made them multi-millionaires; both of these women took risks on themselves.

Lori Greiner, known as both "The QVC Queen" and the warm-blooded shark on "Shark Tank," started out life majoring in journalism and working at *The Chicago Tribune.* While there, she had the inspiration to create an earring holder. Yes, an earring holder. She wanted to solve a problem she faced in those chaotic mornings we all know so well. But she didn't just want one for herself; she realized it was a problem for all jewelry-hoarding women! That may sound silly, but at heart, she knew her idea could improve other women's lives.

Greiner borrowed $300,000 to get started and hustled to get her product into J.C. Penney's in time for holiday shopping. In her first year of business, her company made more than $1 million. Since then, she has created more than 450 products and holds 120 US and international patents. The first secret to her success is her ability to create affordable products that solve everyday problems, and it all started with a messy pile of mismatched earrings on a dresser top. The secret is her belief in herself. She took a risk with that first loan and has become one of the most lauded entrepreneurs of our time—and someone who now helps other women meet success with their business ideas, too.

Greiner's cohort on "Shark Tank," business mogul Barbara Corcoran, also bet on herself, but in her case, it was after more than twenty jobs that didn't work out the way she'd hoped. She started her career as a public-school teacher, a position she kept for just one year. Then she job hopped. Finally, her life changed in one of her least illustrious positions: waiting tables at a diner. She started dating a customer—a home builder in New Jersey—and he ended up loaning her $1,000 to start an apartment rental company. The romance didn't last, but soon the company was doing a half million dollars' worth of real estate sales per year. The ex-boyfriend said she never would have made it without him, which only made her more determined. They divided the business, and she founded the first female-run New York City real estate company, the Corcoran Group, which she sold about twenty-five years later for $66 million. Now, like Greiner, she supports other entrepreneurs, obviously through her television appearances, but also through her website, presentations, and multiple books (my favorite title is *Other Business Lessons I learned from My Mom*).

Whereas I'm not a television personality, I would never have bet the farm on a jewelry holder, and I didn't go through as many jobs as Corcoran did. But I get it. For some of us women, the best risk we can take is on ourselves. Of course, based only on statistics, it might sound crazy to even wager such a bet. In 2021, only *2 percent* of venture capital went to women business founders. Worse, statistics show that women who start with financing from other women find it harder to obtain additional funding down the road. It's a Catch-22. However, I am a contrarian in *so* many ways, and I am proud of it. I see our courage to build financial power as necessary.

Never in my lifetime have women's rights been under threat in the US the way they are now. And, not coincidentally, progress for women in leadership has ground to a halt. American women are vastly underrepresented in elected office, with women making up only 27 percent of Congress despite being 51 percent of our total population.[34] Only 15 percent of the CEOs of Fortune 500 companies are women.[35] Globally, of the 2,668 billionaires compiled in the annual Forbes list, only 327 are women; that's only 12 percent of women in the world who are ultra-rich, many of them from inheritances.[36]

You may have no interest in entrepreneurship but still want a seat at the table when it comes to policies that affect women. As Hillary Clinton

34 "By the Numbers," *Represent Women.* https://www.representwomen.org/current-women-representation#us_overview. Accessed 07/19/2022.
35 Buchholz, Katarina, "How has the number of female CEOs in Fortune 500 companies changed over the last 20 years?" World Economic Forum. 3/10/2022. https://www.weforum.org/agenda/2022/03/ceos-fortune-500-companies-female/ Accessed 7/25/2022.
36 Sandler, Rachel. "The Top Richest Women in the World 2022," *Forbes,* 04/05/22. https://www.forbes.com/sites/rachelsandler/2022/04/05/the-top-richest-women-in-the-world-2022/?sh=5418a0e3446a. Accessed 07/19/2022.

once famously said, "Women's rights are human rights," and I agree. If you're not inclined toward being your own boss, no matter: wealth achieved through investment also brings freedom and power. You may be hard-pressed to believe you could affect change on a national, state, or even local level. But building your own wealth creates a ripple effect. The more of us who figure that out will create bigger waves.

Corcoran and Greiner's confidence and sales abilities are keys to their success, and they are for mine, too, but the business I started in 2020 wasn't foreign to me. Before I decided to go out on my own, I was always engaged in some form of research, starting at the age of fifteen when I entered the sales world. Even then, my first task was to determine my strengths and learn the industry. When I focused my sights on finance, I wasn't truly a newcomer there, either, since my mother had been an investor for as long as I could remember. I'm more comfortable knowing where I'm going before taking a leap, and that's what I want my clients to feel, too. Just like women investors who do better than their male counterparts, I do my research and plenty of research for you, too, come to think of it!

Finance for Women: "Shrink it and Pink it"

Without naming names, there are a lot of highly successful finance coaches and self-labeled gurus out there teaching women what they call financial literacy, but unfortunately, like in subpar schools, they drill only the most basic skills. Conduct a quick Google search for financial coaching for women, and you'll see what I mean. Here are some of the "priceless" gems these coaches share.

Pay down your debt. That advice assumes you have college loans and probably high-interest credit card balances. And if that's the case, there will likely be an entire lecture on how to eliminate that debt and avoid building it again by putting your credit cards in the freezer, deleting shopping apps from your smartphone, or creating and sticking to a precise shopping list. All this while workshops oriented to men teach how to take out credit cards to establish themselves as a good risk, borrow if need be to invest in projects with great ROI (returns on investment) that provides passive income that more than covers paying back that debt down the line. Businesses routinely take on debt to build assets, increase marketing, or avoid taking on shareholders. This advice assumes women are unable to make big, bold decisions with their money.

Start putting money in your 401(k). No kidding. Information on some of these so-called gurus' sites is as basic as defining compound interest, which we are supposed to master in high school algebra. Or how to be careful if someone is offering to double your money. Toss into that grab bag of high finance understanding the Rule of 72. (Okay, maybe that last one has always been a mystery to you, and if so, I'm not being a finance snob. I'm just assuming that someone somewhere along the line explained to you that the Rule of 72 refers to calculating how long it will take for your money to double at a given annual rate of return.) Again, this advice panders to women, suggesting they are financial neophytes.

Write a budget. Seriously? An entire session, chapter, or series of blogs on writing a budget? And women pay for this? Do you see the irony inherent in that? That suggests we need a line in our budget for learning how to write a budget.

Negotiate for a better salary, so you can cover your monthly expenses and have something left to invest. We've all heard the story of the woman who *leaned in* and got a $20,000 raise. What that woman doesn't know is that the guy in the next office is making $40,000 more than she is for the same job, and the CEO is smiling. Would you want to work somewhere that doesn't pay you what you're worth in the first place? While we are on this topic, that *leaning-in* thing is a farce and can backfire as often as it works, if not more so. Sorry, Sheryl Sandburg, but for those of us without HBS degrees and friends like Mark Zuckerberg, it's not the same game. It's not even in the same ballpark.

Cut back on expenses. You know these bits of advice. Get a roommate for your tiny apartment. Live as an extreme frugal warrior, eating nothing but beans and rice and unplugging your toaster when you're not using it—like that kind of minimal savings will give you the edge you're seeking.

Start a side hustle. O. M. G. One of my all-time favorite pieces of crazy-ass advice. Take that knitting hobby you have, honed through the pink pussyhat craze, and launch a shop on Etsy. Use that income to invest, unless you need it to buy carpal tunnel syndrome hand and wrist braces. I'm all for side gigs, but I'm also firmly a proponent of making your money work for you as opposed to working harder for it.

Sure, some of these are common sense steps you need to take before you come meet me, but that's the thing: they're common sense. You don't have to pay $499.95 to attend a weekend-long financial literacy workshop to know those things. Financial gurus pitching workshops to male audiences would never get away with being so limited. Those coaches just assume that the men who come to their workshops or frequent their sites *already have* all these skills. They presume that men are ready to build wealth, to flip real estate, and/or to invest in startups and growing enterprises. Women are completely capable of doing the same.

Of course, you too could start a coaching business teaching common sense. (Get a glam shot for your website.) But it's still not passive income.

You're sweating it out at those weekend workshops and starving yourself to fit in that slinky cocktail wear, plus making TikTok videos at 2:00 a.m. when your kids are asleep. Besides, you're giving out really lame information that, frankly, can be found for free all over the innerwebs. Could you live with yourself? Not to mention, eventually that market will be saturated. It's getting there fast.

Financial Self Care

Another thread in the current explosion of financial coaching for women involves *persuading* you that you're worth it, literally telling you that building wealth isn't selfish or bad but justifiable. The idea is to be prepared for some crisis like your husband leaving you (or dying). Sure, it's true that wealth enables you to have great health care, a livable home, and the ability to retire before you're eighty. No doubt, that is power. But it doesn't have to stop with self-sufficiency.

There's a self-care industry out there that thrives on telling you, "We've got what you need, and you're worth it." The message is right, but the way you achieve what you deserve is not what they have in mind. The benefits of serious wealth go beyond a spa facial and massage, no matter how good they feel. But the message is good, at least as a start. You do deserve what you need. And you deserve to own wealth.

Pooja Lakshmin, a perinatal psychologist who teaches at the George Washington School of Medicine, recently observed in *The New York Times,* "I meet mothers who lean into their guilt like it's a security blanket and hold up their self-sacrifice as a badge of honor …. It's a role that women can inhabit even without a diagnosable mental health condition."[37] That can lead to paying way less attention to your investments than *they* deserve, because you're so busy taking care of everyone else.

So, you've heard it here, once and done: *Do not feel guilty* about growing your own nest egg and more. In fact, just like taking care of yourself, it's best for everyone if you do. In one case, you have enough energy and sanity left to take care of those who are depending on you. In the other, you have the means to support yourself and can enrich other people's lives, too. It's easy to get sucked into the martyr syndrome, sure. As Lakshmin adds, "I don't blame ... mothers for shielding themselves under a cloak of suffering. Appearing too well adjusted is a liability. Leaving your kids in the car for three minutes to get a coffee can be grounds for a call to Child Protective Services and daring to bottle-feed your baby ... can lead to criticism from strangers."[38]

Don't get me wrong: Not all popular financial gurus who charge impressive speaking fees and offer workshops on the above fundamentals are limited or, worse, frauds. One impressive guru who has garnered a great deal of popularity recently is Bola Sokunbi, author of four books about financial pathways to growing your money that are accessible to the least financially savvy reader as well as women who are ready to take the plunge into building real wealth. She's honest about her own early adult financial missteps, which is encouraging for those who think investing is never going to be for them. In her books, she includes interviews with women who have started with practically nothing (or worse) and are well

37 "Mothers Don't Have to Be Martyrs." 5/5/2020. https://www.nytimes.com/2020/05/05/parenting/mothers-not-martyrs.html?auth=login-google1tap&login=google1tap Accessed 7/22/2022.
38 Ibid.

on their way to building wealth. In the aptly named *Grow Your Money*[39], Sokunbi quotes Cindy Zuniga, whose personal story is instructional.

Zuniga, a first-generation American citizen, graduated from law school and landed a job at a prestigious firm, but found herself saddled with about a quarter million dollars of college and grad school debt (of which 90 percent was from law school). Rather than feeling discouraged despite her promising career trajectory, she "went where any Millennial would go" and took an internet deep dive into stories by other women in similar situations, and then moved on to podcasts, blogs, videos, "you name it." She shares on her website that she "was drawn to content created … particularly by women of color, because I found that their stories and journeys resonated with me …. I began my financial freedom journey in January 2016."[40]

Zuniga took all the right first steps. She invested in her firm's 401(k), opened an account with a robo-advisor and scheduled weekly automatic contributions to it, learned about her investment style (she's comfortable as a "passive investor"), and lived modestly but not crazy frugally, budgeting so well that she became debt-free in four years. Granted, she had a great starting salary as a litigator, but still, many people could have blown all that on Manolos and Manipedis. Today she has a well-diversified portfolio, continually increases the amounts she contributes, and is well on her way to becoming a savvy investor.

When Sokunbi asked why investing is so important to her, Zuniga said, "My parents immigrated to this country with practically nothing … They weren't able to teach me about investing because they were too busy putting food on the table …. I want to build real generational wealth so

39 *Grow Your Money.* Hoboken, NJ: Wiley and Sons, 2021.
40 https://www.zero-basedbudget.com/about. Accessed 7/22/2022.

that my children and my children's children will never lack and will benefit from the seeds I plant today."[41] She follows a rule she calls 10—40—50: living off 50 percent of her income, donating 10 percent, and investing the rest. Zuniga sets a great example for others. In building wealth, she's not only doing it for herself. She's doing it for subsequent generations, too, in the best possible way.

That's part of what I mean by power: having enough money to influence others' lives and futures, including those of your kids, their kids, your friends, your local community, the country (yes, the country—more on that in a bit), and the future in general. Yes, having money can influence your—and our—world. That world that sometimes seems like it's burning down faster than the people who are supposed to be keeping it safe can "create narratives" that make them look responsible. We can't rely on those people. They're the ones who got us into this mess, and the vast majority of them are old white men, just like the guys who run the finance world. Ahh! See the connection?

Money Really Does Buy Power

To grasp how much of an influence we can have, consider first the small scale. If you are financially independent, that means others in your family do not have purse power, aka that "I'm paying, so you'll do as I say" line we've all heard that makes us want to scream. You know, "I'd love to help you buy a house, but only if you buy …" Insert in your parents' voices, "the one I think you should have in the neighborhood I think is right for you." Or "Sure, honey, if you want to re-do the guest room as your office, that's great, but since I make the bigger salary, let's first turn our garage into

41 Bokundi, op cit, pp. 48-50.

the man cave I've been wanting so I'm not too stressed to stay at the top of my game."

Stand up for your wealth, and you're standing up for yourself. And Maya Angelou once said, "Every time a woman stands up for herself... she stands up for all women."[42] We're in this together.

Next, think about the community in which you live. Your neighbor, who has ideas you agree with, is running for school board. You can support her campaign. Your local YWCA needs funding for a project you like that will help girls. You can donate to the cause. A few of your friends are putting together a business startup right in your community that will change your life for the better—think modestly, if you will, like a new yoga studio or the coziest cafe or indie bookstore you can imagine. Maybe they're going to save the local downtown movie theater but can only do that with financial support from the community; it's not your partner's thing, but you adore the place and want to help out. Whatever the cause, whatever your passion, if you have the means, you can contribute more than just volunteer hours. And even your volunteer hours can be more numerous, because, guess what? With passive income supplementing your freelance gig, you don't have to put in as many hours.

My theory is that if women were in charge, we'd be in less of a dumpster in terms of climate, human rights, and democracy. Why? Because, as much as we might hate to admit it, we women are biologically wired, honed through millennia of raising children, to have that caregiving urge. What better way to nurture others than to build up enough wealth and power to influence the bigger picture?

42 AZ Quotes. https://www.azquotes.com/quote/502609. Accessed 7/22/2022.

Recently, my partner and I went car shopping. We walked into the dealership on a Saturday, and I asked to work with a sales*woman*. The sales*man* looked nervously at another sales*man* and said, "Oh, our sales-*woman* isn't in today." It was a Saturday, the busiest day in a car dealership. I pointed that out to the men who were staring at me like I had three heads, and they had no excuse. Of course, they didn't have a woman salesperson. We left because we had the money to buy a vehicle and wanted to spend it at a dealership where women matter. We should all be doing that.

In France, if a company hires a man, it also has to hire a woman at the same salary, or it's subject to a fine. That's parity. In Germany and Sweden, women receive paid benefits for up to two years after having a baby and are assured a job at the same firm when they're ready to return. Men are also eligible for paid paternity leave. That's parity, too.

But my goal isn't parity. It's a total takeover! Only partly kidding. Imagine what the world would be like if the genetically wired caregiver gender comprised the majority of the 1 percent.

MacKenzie Scott revealed in December 2020 that she had donated "$4.2 billion of her fortune in the preceding four months—on top of the $1.7 billion she had given away earlier in 2020." And she did so in "mainly no-strings-attached messaging accompanying the gifts." Plus, she moved *fast*. She signed The Giving Pledge in 2019 less than two months after her divorce from Jeff Bezos was finalized.[43] That means she has committed to "give half of her $35 billion in assets, or at least $17 billion, to charity over

43 The Giving Pledge was founded by Warren Buffett, Melinda French Gates, and Bill Gates, but the Gates Foundation is not a "no-strings attached" organization—in fact, quite the reverse.

her lifetime or in her will."[44] Scott's ex-husband may be the wealthiest man in the world, but he doesn't share well.[45]

According to *The New York Times,* "Philanthropy watchers lauded Ms. Scott's speed, the research she put into her decisions … and the wide scope of her chosen beneficiaries, which included historically Black colleges and universities, community colleges, and Y.M.C.A. and Y.W.C.A. organizations."[46] She was committed to education and other causes that benefit women and families—she put herself through Princeton after her family suffered setbacks making it impossible for them to do so—so she knew what she wanted to support. And as remarkable as Scott is, she is only one in a long line of women philanthropists who, research shows, give nearly twice as much as men do.[47]

Right now, we need to be taking care of ourselves well, because then we can take care of other women well, which means taking care of the world well. It's ironic, really: if men (and, certainly, more than a few women) think changing Roe v. Wade will actually help the US, they are sorely mistaken. Even beyond the harm sure to come to so many women from the Supreme Court's recent Dobbs Case, "enforced pregnancy" will keep women out of the workforce, which is without question part of what the movement to end choice has been about since the 1970s. Just think what vast numbers of women out of the workforce would do not only to their and their families' lives but also to the US economy. As Sheila Holkatar wrote in May 2022

---

44 Theodore Schleifer, "MacKenzie [Scott] Bezos signed the philanthropic commitment her exhusband spurted." Vox. 5/28/2019. https://www.vox.com/recode/2019/5/28/18641623/mackenzie-bezos-giving-pledge-philanthropy-jeff-bezos-divorce Accessed 7/22/2022.

45 Ibid.

46 Ibid.

47 "Safronova, op cit.

in *The New Yorker,* research conducted in the 1970s showed that women "who were able to delay motherhood through legal access to abortion were much more likely to finish college, pursue higher degrees, spend longer in the labor force, and enter higher-paying occupations; they were much less likely to fall into poverty later in life."[48] The same holds true for a change in access to contraception, should that be the next women's rights issue the Supreme Court takes up.

Ruth Bader Ginsberg once said, "Women belong in all places where decisions are being made." If we want to roll back recent attacks on women's rights, and make lasting progress, we need to rise to the occasion. Many women clients don't think of themselves as risk takers, and we need to get over that. Wait, you say? The statistics about women getting better returns on investment suggest that we're risk-averse, right?

Consider this: What guy do you know would risk unprotected sex if he were the one who might get pregnant?

So yes, we can do it too. Now is our time. We need to build and invest in women's businesses. That's all we should be doing.

First, we need to get to know ourselves as investors. What are our identifiable objectives? What kind of diversification are we after? Do we like real estate, or capital investing, and if the latter, start-ups or growth? What kind of risk takers are we?

We'll take a look at determining those answers in the next chapter.

---

48 "The Devastating Effects of an Abortion Ban." *The New Yorker,* 5/11/2022. https://www.newyorker.com/business/currency/the-devastating-economic-impacts-of-an-abortion-ban Accessed 7/25/2022.

CHAPTER FIVE

Understanding Alternatives

The 2015 film *The Big Short* (and the book on which it's based) accomplished three remarkable things. (1) It made the world of Wall Street entertaining. (2) It explained the convoluted financial instruments of the early 2000s that were previously understood only by the Dark Lords of the finance industry: big banks, hedge funds, and brokerage services. (3) It turned rebels who refused to worship at the altar of high finance into superheroes. Their powers? Diligence and eyes able to pierce the cloud of greed obscuring the Dark Lords' citadels.

These whip-smart guys (and all of them were *guys*) recognized, through regular old financial analyst drudgery (combing through financial statements and diving deeply into due diligence), that there was a false sense of enthusiasm in the air about mortgage-backed securities. It was like savvy investors and normally cautious money managers were not only teetering on cliffs above a shimmering ocean below, but also jumping in feet first, so high on anticipation and avarice that they didn't see that it was way shallower than it looked from up there. Then they crashed right into the rocky hazards below.

The film is based on real-life investors and market analysts Steve Eisman, Michael Burry, Greg Lippmann, Charlie Ledley, Jamie Mai, and Ben Hockett, who figured out that the popular subprime mortgage-backed investment instruments selling like hotcakes were actually worthless. The instruments were "derivatives," assets based on other assets, none of them tangible. Don't let the lingo frighten you, especially because you won't have to remember it for long. Collateralized debt obligations (CDOs) were basically repackaged bundles of mortgages that had been issued to home buyers who were destined to default. Why did investors fall for them and buy in? Simple. The "instruments" received inflated ratings from credit rating agencies (such as the once historically respected but now less trusted Moody's and S&P). Our superheroes realized that once the interest rates on these mortgages started rising, making them unaffordable even to homebuyers working with lax lenders, or housing prices stopped rising due to a slowdown in demand, or both, the bonds and CDOs would be as poisonous to the financial system as nuclear waste was to Chernobyl.

Here comes the rub. These investors—who, by the way, weren't all working together but came to their realizations somewhat independently—figured out how to profit from the whole mess. They could bet against, or *short*, in Wall Street terms, this heap of soon-to-be-worthless paper. They issued *swaps*, which were like an insurance policy: the buyer paid regular premiums to the seller, but if the housing market collapsed, the seller would have to pay the full value of the policy. Clever, don't you think? When the inevitable happened, investors would scramble to buy this "insurance coverage" against their devalued bonds and CDOs. Not to be crude, but it was like a spouse buying dirt cheap life insurance on a husband in the last stages of pancreatic cancer.

These clever, contrarian superheroes figured out how to make oodles of cash off greed and colossal shortsightedness. The book and film exposed the irrationality of modern capitalism when driven by the greediest bastards on Wall Street in cahoots with their slimy ex-patriots at the Fed. Yet, the bad guys—and I again mean 99 percent *guys*—continue to this day to wield the most economic and political power in America.

And the superheroes who ran the big short? They certainly did not lose their homes like the 10 million Americans who were foreclosed on between 2007 and 2014. In fact, you can rest assured that they will never have to worry about retirement.

To those 10 million unfortunate home buyers, the Great Recession was way more than a movie, and it was to investors, too. The financial crisis of 2007-2008 changed the way many investors look at the market, and not just in terms of mortgage-based security madness. Not since the Depression of the 1930s had the saying, "In times of crisis, all correlations go to one," felt more true. The maxim means that when there's a panic and everyone is rushing to the exits—most recently witnessed during the initial spread of COVID-19—all stocks are punished equally and indiscriminately. Every investor who has been in the market for a while has seen this "sell first, ask questions later" exodus.

The saying refers to the hard-earned wisdom that typical portfolio diversification isn't going to help an investor during the worst of times, when she needs "downside protection." In the disaster of 2007—2008, just as in 2020, individual price drops weren't related to industry—they all fell as a group. In other words, the origin of the sell-off doesn't matter. Eventually, everything is crashing. It's particularly unsettling when these events are global. In 2007-2008 and in 2020, investors who thought they were safe due to diversification through international stocks weren't immune. It's a very unpleasant lesson to learn.

In 2020, this contrarian, yours truly, was busy opening her own business and making it possible for her clients to invest in alt funds—alternative investments, or basically anything not tied to indexes, interest rates, or the markets. Alts behave differently from market-based assets and are thus less volatile when the market is.

There are drawbacks to alts. One thing that makes investors new to alts nervous is that they're relatively illiquid. But, like I said, when there is high market volatility, alternative investments can perform very differently from the more liquid stock and bond markets. Between February 19th and February 27th of 2020, US diversified stock funds lost between 10.8 and 11.6 percent. Now that's some chaos that will bring on despair—and more run-for-the-hills style panic. Of course, not all alternative investments outperformed in 2020; some underperformed, and when that happens, investors in alts need to remember that illiquidity can be as psychologically challenging as volatile markets. But this same illiquidity can be a boon, because if you're invested only in stocks and bonds that are plummeting, you're not going to have the resources to enjoy the fruits of future bull markets. Including alts in your portfolio not only limits drawdowns but also enhances long-term returns. Plus, you, as the investor, don't feel like you're in a rodeo run by drunken cowboys.

In this chapter, I'd like to give you a basic introduction to the unique aspects of alternative investments (both the advantages and disadvantages), as well as the major types of alts and my preferences among them.

Then we'll look at some real-world examples to recover from the abstract craziness with which I began this chapter. One of the main reasons I like alts, beyond their high returns on investment (ROIs) is that they're tangible. You don't need to parse them to understand them. Sure, you need to research them and understand what your equity is supporting, but imagine the pleasure of being able to visualize the products and/or services in which you're invested.

What Are Alts?

There's no official definition of alts, sometimes referred to as "non-traditional assets" or "direct investments." In general, the term means "investments outside of the traditional asset classes of publicly traded stocks, bonds, and cash, including the 'wrappers' that hold those traditional asset classes" (like Exchange Traded Funds [ETFs], mutual funds, and index funds).[49] Alts have been around since before the Medicis commissioned Lorenzo Ghiberti to sculpt the "Gates of Paradise" for the Baptistry of San Giovanni in Florence. Of course, the gentry and royalty's paintings, castles, and sculptures were secure investments, despite having no one to sell them to. Even if you were newly bourgeois, it was tough to break into that "market." The alts market today can be just as opaque. So, what if you're interested in the palace jewels and have the resources to buy them? You're not buying bronze doors from Florence. What can you purchase?

Alts also have varied characteristics: most offer a combined return including both an income stream, even if it's small, and price appreciation. These include private equity funds, Real Estate Investment Trusts (REITs),

---

49 Atkinson, Jimmy, and Andy Hagans, *The Investor's Guide to Alternative Investments,* Alternative Investors Database. https://altsdb.com/wp-content/uploads/2022/04/The-Investors-Guide-To-Alternative-Investments.pdf Accessed 8/15/2022

and Business Development Companies (BDCs). More on these later. There are also purely speculative alts: assets that produce no income and whose ROI is price appreciation only. Precious metals, commodities, and investment-grade collectibles and artwork fall into that latter category. Oh, and the palace jewels.

Because alts are relatively illiquid compared to stocks and bonds, investors expect to hold them for five to ten years. That's not to say you could not liquidate your investment, but if you did, you'd likely experience some financial pain, or what the boys on Wall Street call "a haircut." But alts are illiquid in a couple of different ways:

- An alternative investment sponsor will offer to buy back an individual investor's shares, but is limited to buying back a certain amount and will only pay a discounted price.

- The alt will have an existing secondary market, but the secondary market will be quite "thin," with buyers demanding a significant discount to provide liquidity to potential sellers. It's considerably more difficult to sell a 100-year-old bottle of French wine, for example, than 100 shares of IBM.

- Investors may even have difficulty valuing their investments if the asset is super rare; one example on Investopedia is a 1933 Saint-Gaudens Double Eagle $20 gold coin, as there are only thirteen known to exist and only one can be legally owned.[50]

50 Chen, James, "Alternative Investment," *Investopedia.com*, updated 2/26/22. https://www.investopedia.com/terms/a/alternative_investment.asp Accessed 8/12/2022

Another difference between alts and traditional investing is that you can buy into that IBM stock with minimal cash on hand. That has never been true for alts funds, which since their inception have been available to institutional or accredited investors.[51] Furthermore, alts are neither publicly traded nor public, which means they do not have to be registered with the Securities and Exchange Commission (SEC) or the Commodity Futures Trading Commission (CFTC). Nonetheless, sponsors of private alts (like me) are subject to financial reporting regulations at the state level and to federal and state anti-fraud regulations. A true positive of my fund is that I'm a fiduciary, which means I'm *legally bound* to put your interests ahead of mine. Your investment may be less liquid, but you can rest assured that you and your goals are my number one priority.

Lastly, there's a level of sophistication associated with alts that isn't present with investing in stocks and bonds. Although, as I mentioned, they're not like those early 2000s devilish financial tongue twisters you'll likely never wrap your head around (and are often designed exactly for that purpose), you will have to do a bit more research to feel comfortable and understand your investment than you would if you were buying shares in Apple or a well-known mutual fund. It's not the underlying investment that can be confusing, even though you'll want to get to know it. It's more the "wrapper" on alts like REITs or Delaware Statutory Trusts (DSTs).

Both REITs and DSTs own and lease commercial real estate and have relatively simple business models. But they also have unique legal and structural aspects that can be deceiving. I'm not a fan of either, because

51 Accredited investors must have a net worth of at least $1 million, excluding the value of their primary residence, or have income of at least $200,000/year for the prior two years, or $300,000 combined if married, plus the expectation to earn at least the same amount in the current year.

in the fine print, you'll probably discover that you aren't the one making decisions about your investment, and you will be the last person to be paid when the fund generates income. Those making the decisions will reap the benefits (particularly the tax benefits in most cases), and you'll be catching the crumbs. In addition, REITs and DSTs are subject to influences from interest rates and other factors, and, as such, are more correlated to traditional asset classes.

Other types of alts can also be confusing to the investor in similar ways. For example, energy programs may be structured as limited partnerships, with one or more general partners (GPs) who actively manage the underlying investments and many limited partners (LPs) who are passive investors. Like REITs and DSTs, limited partnerships are governed by contracts meant to benefit the sponsors. Understanding these unique aspects requires you to perform research and can seem like a daunting hurdle. After all, your cousin works for IBM, your dad has shares of IBM, etc. Stocks and bonds seem a lot easier, market volatility aside.

But you are a woman and love research, right? Or at least feel better when you've done it, just like with a Pilates class. And, if you were or are frightened of it, that was before you met me.

Other Alts to Avoid

So I have warned you to stay away from REITs and DSTs with fine print in the contracts that will reduce your return. What else is on my no-go list? I've mentioned NFTs before, but let's address them again here.

Remember how the acronym NFT stands for "non-fungible token"? Does it sound as much like alien language as derivatives and collateralized debt obligations? With a sort of mushroomy twist? Indeed, they're intangible. Similar to cryptocurrencies like Bitcoin, NFTs are digital assets that are purchased, sold, and traded at will, just like physical assets reminiscent of our landed gentry and their tapestries (although the market for tapestries has probably waned). Where does the word "token" come in? Each one is unique and attached to a digital certificate of ownership that proves it. And how about "fungible"? That basically translates to "exchangeable"—in this case, for something similar or equal in value. A non-fungible asset is one-of-a-kind and has no equivalent. The Mona Lisa, for example, is non-fungible. However, it's not digital, either, and unless you're a skilled cat burglar, you're never getting your hands on it.

NFTs, on the other hand, are all too easily purchased—and very tempting. They are sold through *blockchains*, or databases that store various pieces of digital information—the blocks—in chronological order. They're decentralized, which means their control is spread across different entities, which allows buyers and sellers to deal directly with one another instead of working through a middleman. When you purchase your digital asset, it's recorded in a public blockchain ledger accessible by millions of computers worldwide that serves as proof of ownership and value.

You've heard that NFTs are selling for thousands and even millions of dollars. Yes, and the sales themselves are fueling the craze. Many digital artists have sold original artwork or songs for multiple millions of dollars. For example, the Canadian songwriter Grimes sold two videos for more than $6 million. One NFT out there is the very first Tweet, which in 2022 was worth about $2.5 million. But the entire phenomenon should give you pause. When one of the most highly valued NFTs out there is an exclusive collection of digital apes, each with its own unique look and traits, you know you're in unfamiliar territory. And when one of the metaverses offering "property" and "goods" is called *Sandbox?* That gives you an idea of what's happening here. I'd prefer not to play in one. As of this writing,

FTX, one of the largest crypto-exchange platforms (valued at $32 billion as of November 2022), filed for bankruptcy, leaving thousands of investors without recourse. Crypto investments aren't backed by the FDIC, so whatever investors lose is as good as dust in the wind. It also appears FTX's CEO, Sam Bankman Fried, used investor money to prop up and cover the obligations of his own separate company, which was trading on risky bets. It smells criminal because it probably is.

And Now, Private Equity

Private equity (PE) is a broad category that refers to capital investment made into private companies, or those not listed on a public exchange, such as the New York Stock Exchange. There are several subsets of private equity, including:

- Venture capital, which focuses on startup and early-stage ventures;
- Growth capital, which helps more mature companies expand or restructure;
- Buyouts occur when a company or one of its divisions is purchased outright.

An important aspect of PE is the relationship between the investing firm and the company receiving capital. Private equity companies often provide more than just capital to the firms they invest in; they also provide benefits like industry expertise, talent sourcing assistance, and mentorship to founders.

Venture capital is the riskiest of these three because, by its nature, a startup has no track record. You can use comparable companies to estimate returns, but you're dealing with a lot of unknowns. I prefer private equity growth capital in industries I've worked in and know inside and out, like oil and gas, but also in new areas like coffee, cannabis, and innovative new types of energy.

The early history of private equity traces back to Pittsburgh in 1901, when J.P. Morgan bought Carnegie Steel Company from Andrew Carnegie and Henry Phipps for $480 million, the first trade on what would become the private equity market we know today. Phipps founded his own trust in 1907 to invest his millions in private businesses and exclusive holdings. But it wasn't until after World War II, when the first venture capital firms were founded, that private equity became more well-known, and even through the 1970s, it was only a small portion of portfolios (if at all), despite the fantastic returns it was bringing to high-end investors.

Two of the earliest venture capital firms were established in 1946: American Research and Development Corp. (ARD) and J.H. Whitney & Company. ARD was founded by Georges Doriot, the "father of venture capitalism," whose greatest investment was inarguably Digital Equipment Corp., which he bought for $70,000 and sold for $37 million—an increase of 52,757 percent. Then, President Dwight D. Eisenhower enacted the Small Business Act of 1958, which allowed venture capital firms, known as "Small Business Investment Companies" (SBICs), to borrow money from the government at below-market interest rates in order to invest in entrepreneurial ventures. It was the Cold War, and through this plan, Eisenhower was able to increase technological advances in the race against the Soviets. Before long, independent venture capital firms established themselves as major players. They were not dependent on government support; they offered more flexibility, something investors loved. These companies rapidly outpaced SBICs.

Knowing the history makes PE seem even more patriotic. It really is, because your dollars are supporting small and medium-sized businesses, which in turn are growing the American economy.

Another related historical tidbit is the story of a quiet man known as the "spiritual father" of private equity. Jerome Kohlberg, the son of an importer and a veteran of WWII, earned an MBA from Harvard and a JD from Columbia, then joined Bear Stearns. There, he became the antithesis of the corporate raider. By fostering the type of private equity known as leveraged buyouts (LBOs), he made it possible for owners and employees of companies to retain control when vultures circled around their vulnerable, debt-laden companies. Known for terming the purchase of any company with more than 50 percent debt "ungentlemanly," he was the odd man out at Bear Stearns and eventually left to found his own company, Kohlberg & Son, and later Kohlberg Kravitz Roberts. In the 1980s, when his own junior partners became the *Barbarians at the Gate* described by investigative journalists Byran Burrough and John Helyar, Kohlberg left again. They'd turned the LBO into a vehicle as destructive as corporate raids themselves, and he wanted none of it. LBOs' reputation has since been restored, as has that of private equity; both are now known for helping companies achieve more profit while keeping their leadership intact. A 2015 profile in *Money Week* published after Kohlberg's passing stated, "It is one of the great Wall Street ironies that Bear Stearns, which dismissed [Kohlberg's] LBO model, no longer exists—while the tiny outfit he began with just $120,000 is 'one of the world's premier investment firms.'"[52]

It's important to acknowledge that not everyone sings the praises of private equity. A 2020 article on the website *Vox* recounts the sad tale of Toys-R-Us and the failure of their private investors to save the company (although a comeback is underway through a partnership with Macy's, and who hasn't missed Geoffrey the Giraffe?!). The article lists other companies that went belly up despite private investment: Payless Shoes, Shopko, and RadioShack. Individuals like performing artists have also complained. Taylor Swift, for example, blames battles over her songs on what she calls the "unregulated world of private equity."[53] But how much of these companies' demise or independents' issues were and are impossible to prevent? Is it fair to say that private equity squeezes profit out of companies, or is it truer that without private investment, companies would have no opportunity to grow and blossom? I believe the latter.

Two years after founding Alternative Wealth Partners (AWP), we have over 25 individual portfolio companies, we are managing 4 private equity funds, and paying dividends to investors. We've invested in oil & gas, real estate, manufacturing companies and other consumer goods businesses. These businesses generate millions of dollar worth of revenue and profit on behalf of our funds. Those returns don't come from failing companies.

---

52 "The "Spiritual Father" of private equity who favored integrity over hardball tactics," *Money Week,* August 14, 2015. https://kohlbergfoundation.org/files/2015/09/Money-Week-7.pdf Accessed September 1, 2022.

53 Stewart, Emily, "What is private equity, and why is it killing everything you love?" *Vos,* January 6, 2020. https://www.vox.com/the-goods/2020/1/6/21024740/private-equity-taylor-swift-toys-r-us-elizabeth-warren Accessed September 5, 2022.

There's one other caveat about PE that it would be irresponsible to leave unmentioned: some private equity investments can be relatively risky due to independent factors, and sometimes past performance is not indicative of future performance. But when you work with us, you know what you're getting into. We know the industries so well that we add value to the companies in which we invest; we serve as advisors as well as investors. I mean, if you're invested in Microsoft, you're not going to be able to walk into headquarters and say, "Hey, I have a great idea that can enhance revenues." We work with companies we can help and professionals who want to listen to our expertise. And I've found that female investors like this aspect of private equity.

Of course, nothing is failsafe. There could always be a financial crisis or macroeconomic event with unexpected results. But we remain on top of forecasts and trends and have been successful in avoiding downturns.

You might wonder if you fit the profile of someone who is drawn to PE or whether you're ready. I use an analogy to help clients figure that out.

Let's say you're out for lunch and ask your waiter for a Coke, your go-to, and he says, "Sorry, we don't have Coke, but we have Pepsi." Coke drinkers generally don't like Pepsi, and vice versa, am I right? So you decide that water is fine. But what would you do if your waiter said, "We don't have Coke, but we do have this great new artisanal soda line," and rattled off a bunch of choices you'd never heard of before. Intriguing, right? So you take a risk and try the new soda, and you love it. In fact, it's even better than Coke. You've just expanded your options, and your day is richer for it.

Later, you hear that the artisanal soda company is doing well and thinking of expanding to a national market. You're invested in Coca-Cola, and because the company is well run, your returns have been predictable, and you could cash out basically any time. But you have tasted this soda, and you like that it has probiotics in it. You've bought six-packs of it at Kroger for months now, and when you met the founders recently at a networking event, you knew instantly they were going places. After some more detailed research, your gut says that returns will be huge if you buy in now and are patient. You don't have to sell your Coca-Cola stock, but you have the opportunity to invest in something new that's likely to grow by leaps and bounds, appeal to a new and bigger market, and pay you better rewards. That means you're ready.

Some people would just put more money into Coca-Cola, and that's fine, too. Everyone has different styles and risk tolerances. Lack of liquidity and different risks can make new investors in private equity squeamish. But remember that these risks demand a premium: higher returns on investment. Investors who understand their risk tolerance and feel comfortable with where they're putting their money will reap higher long-term rewards. The variance in returns is linked to the performance of the specific underlying investment as well as the skill of the sponsor's management team.

I'm proud of my record and my team. I like to think that we continue in the tradition of Kohlberg and the guys in *The Big Short* (who I get to work with today!), today's superheroes, providing private equity to companies with solid growth prospects while simultaneously enriching our clients.

Advantages

- Access to previously unavailable asset classes.
- Many assets held by alternative investments are newly available to non-institutional investors.

- Hedging against inflation and economic headwinds.

- Some (but not all) alts will outperform traditional investments during periods of high inflation, macroeconomic instability, or recession.

- Diversification and total portfolio returns.

- Reduced tax liability: Many alternative investments, such as energy programs offer investors significant tax benefits.

Disadvantages

- Illiquidity: The liquidity of different types of alts varies significantly, but they are generally less liquid than traditional investments. Some alts may be illiquid for 10 years or more. For many types of alts, there is a limited or non-existent secondary market, and cashing out early may require that the investor take a significant haircut.

- Complexity: Alts are generally (but not always) more complex and less widely understood than traditional investments like stocks, bonds, and mutual funds. An alts investor must be willing to perform significant research and due diligence in the market segment in which he or she plans to invest.

- Fees: The fees associated with many types of alts are relatively similar to those of any actively managed investment. In general, fees for alts are higher than those associated with a passively managed traditional investment, such as an index fund. But if you are working with a fiduciary like me, your interests are prioritized.

Should You Include Alternative Investments In Your Portfolio?

Alts are an asset "super class," containing many different types of investments. Depending on the specific type of alt in question, it may or may not be an appropriate investment for you. That being said, here are some general guidelines that you may want to keep in mind as you review your portfolio construction. Alts are potentially worth including in the portfolio of an investor who:

- is an accredited investor,
- is comfortable with an investment life cycle of five to ten years and illiquidity during that life cycle,
- is willing and able to engage in significant research and due diligence for prospective investments, for comfort's sake—or, even better, enjoys it!
- is interested in the diversification benefits that alts offer,
- has recently had a significant capital gain and/or is interested in tax advantages.

Alts should probably <u>not</u> be included in the portfolio of an investor who is NOT:

- an accredited investor,

- able or willing to tie up cash for a five-to-ten-year life cycle, during which an investment would be generally illiquid,
- unwilling or unable to perform significant research and due diligence for prospective investments,
- seeking to actively reduce tax liability from investment returns (although, why wouldn't you be?),
- invested all or most of their investment assets inside tax-advantaged accounts such as IRAs or 401(k)s, therefore negating the potential tax advantages of certain alts.

$

CHAPTER SIX

Time to Stop Whitewashing the Financial Industry

It was January 13, 2020, and at the offices of the famed Hollywood news outlet *Deadline,* staff were waiting with bated breath to hear the nominees for the Oscars. Later that morning, reporter Dino-Ray Ramos wrote about the experience.

> One by one, [Issa Rae] announced the nominees: "*The Irishman*, Martin Scorsese; *Joker,* Todd Phillips; *1917,* Sam Mendes; *Once Upon a Time in Hollywood,* Quentin Tarantino..." and finally, "*Parasite,* Bong Joon Ho." After she listed the names, she said, "Congratulations to those men"—which pretty much says it all.[54]

54 Ramons, Dino-Ray. "Hollywood Heated Over Oscar Snub for Female Directions." *Deadline.* January 13, 2020. https://deadline.com/2020/01/women-directors-snubbed-2020-oscar-nominations-the-farewell-lulu-wang-little-women-greta-gerwig-honey-boy-alma-harel-1202829533/ Accessed September 26, 2022.

Published that afternoon, the article's headline was: "Hollywood Heated Over Oscar Snub For Female Directors."[55]

Still later that day, Kirsten Schaffer, Executive Director of the LA organization Women in Film, released a statement in regard to the lack of women in the Best Director category:

> It's disheartening that even as the number of women nominated for awards in documentary, short film, and technical categories increases, there have still only been five women considered for the Best Directing award in its ninety-two-year history. The Academy has made efforts to balance its voting bodies, but gender equality and diversity do not just happen. Without deep systemic change in the industry and a real commitment to equity in film finance, distribution, and marketing, this bleak trend will continue.[56]

So, when Jane Campion became the third woman to win the prize in 2022, the number of women directors who won Oscars increased by 200 percent! That's the thing about statistics. By 2022, only seven women directors had been nominated, and only three had walked away with statuettes. But that percent increase sure looks impressive!

Hollywood insiders continue to make a lot of noise about how only about 3 percent of Oscars awarded to directors have gone to women. Because they have, change is now happening, even if it seems to be happening only in sporadic grand gestures. The point is that members of the

55 Ibid.
56 Ibid.

industry are drawing attention to the industry's diversity and inclusion problems.

Where is the outrage in the financial industry that in 2020, the last year for which we have figures, big bank and global financial company C-suites were only 11 percent women? One headline in *Barron's* screams that in 2020, "Women in Financial Services C-suites Rose 10 percent In The Past Five Years."[57] But remember the 200 percent increase in female directors winning Oscars? Considering women made up only 10 percent of all the financial industry's largest firms' C-suites in 2015, those are hardly numbers that indicate real progress. Plus, the pandemic reversed even that paltry increase at those firms.

That's not to say that there haven't been different *types* of progress for women in finance. It's just that you haven't read about the women who are forging new paths. Reporters in the finance industry have noticed them, but these stories fail to make it into the mainstream news. We have been creative and innovative, and it goes unnoticed. We don't get an Oscar for what we're doing. At least not yet. That doesn't mean we don't deserve it. There are a lot of fantastic women doing things in the finance industry that are welcoming to the women clients who weren't valued in those old-school environments.

But first, let's take a look at the state of women employees at the big financial firms, which in turn determines the types of services available to diverse women clients in the grand scheme of things.

---

57 Norton, Leslie P. "Women in Financial-Services C-Suites Rose 10% Over Past Five Years." Barron's, March 11, 2021. https://www.barrons.com/articles/women-in-financial-services-c-suite-rose-10-in-past-five-years-51615480290 Accessed September 22, 2022.

Finance Industry v. Corporate America

Lean In, the organization founded by Sheryl Sandberg in conjunction with her 2013 book of the same name, is a great resource for statistics on women in the workforce. The data Lean In collected in another 2019 study shows that women lag behind men in all of corporate America, and, unsurprisingly, women of color are even farther behind. For all the corporate publicity around Diversity, Equity, and Inclusion (DEI), very little changes in the larger companies, and often it's two steps forward, one step back, or worse.

According to the Lean In site, across the board, women (both white and minority) represented 17 percent of the C-suite in 2017, and 21 percent in 2019—by 2019, more than double that correlative statistic in the financial industry.[58] In entry-level positions, women made up 45 percent of the workforce in 2018, compared to 48 percent in 2019. Obviously, something is happening along the way, and it's not the "glass ceiling" we've all talked about for decades. The "broken rung of the ladder," as the Lean In site refers to it, is between entry level and management: 48 percent of employees are women at the entry level, but only 38 percent in management. It's down to 30 percent by the senior vice president level. In summary, about half of the corporate world is made up of women at the entry level, which sinks to less than a third by top-level management. And the figures are worse in finance.

Sheryl Sandberg was Chief Operating Officer at Facebook, now Meta Platforms, and LeanIn.org says the group's mission is to "help women achieve their ambitions and work to create an equal world."[59] Yet, according

58 https://leanin.org/women-in-the-workplace-2019. Accessed September 24, 2022.
59 Ibid.

to a 2020 report on DEI in the finance industry by the House Committee on Financial Services, guess how many of Facebook's asset managers were women in that year. I'll give you a hint: according to McKinsey & Co., the numbers of women in asset management lag behind even those in other sectors of the financial services industry.[60]

The number is zero. In 2020, Facebook had not one female asset manager.[61]

Pandemic Pain

Of course, we are all hyperaware of what happened to women in the workforce from 2020 to 2022. Take, for example, this story from Jenny, whom I met at a networking event years ago. She was making a very nice six-figure salary for a large financial firm in Dallas when she quit her job in December 2019 to move; her husband, Neil, was relocating for a job with the New York office of the huge law firm where he works. She was being wooed for the C-suite at a mid-size venture capital firm (when you add small and midsize finance companies to the mix, it was estimated in 2020 that women made up 24 percent of C-suites) and planned to be working there as soon as she got settled, but she was still enrolling her daughters in school and switching over her driver's license and registration when COVID hit and everything shut down.

In 2021, the company that had wooed her—she was so far along in talks that they'd been negotiating compensation packages—told her they

60 https://www.mckinsey.com/industries/financial-services/our-insights/closing-the-gender-and-race-gaps-in-north-american-financial-services

61 "Diversity and Inclusion: Holding Americans Large Banks Accountable." Report Prepared by the Majority Staff of the Committee on Financial Services, U.S. House of Representatives. 2020. https://financialservices.house.gov/issues/diversity-and-inclusion-holding-america-s-large-banks-accountable.htm Accessed September 26, 2022.

were reorganizing as many "female employees were shifting responsibilities so they could be at home more." Suddenly, they weren't sure where she'd be the best fit—even though she hadn't expressed any wish to work from home.

"I knew what women must have felt like in the 1950s," Jenny said, "when companies assumed that it made no sense to hire someone who would only stay with them until she had kids."

Human Resources and the partner who had wanted to hire her promised her an answer by the end of 2021. But in September 2022, with Neil well-ensconced in his new position, she still had no new job. Neil wasn't complaining. With his more intense hours, it was convenient for her to be home with the kids; they didn't have to worry about childcare when COVID or other random issues reared their ugly heads; and he had a larger salary that more than made up for the higher expenses in Manhattan. Jenny told me she was sinking into confusion and despair.

"I'm not even sure I want to continue working outside the home," Jenny said, "especially because I don't trust this new firm anymore, and I thought its culture was one of the better ones."

As reported in *Fortune* magazine in February 2022, two years after the COVID lockdown began, "Plenty of people have gone back to work, but the women's workforce participation rate has not recovered."[62] That's not only because of home demands; it's also because women were frustrated before the pandemic. According to 2021 McKinsey & Company findings,

---

62 Forman, Tami. "Women's Workforce Participation Has Plummeted." *Fortune*. February 2, 2022. https://fortune.com/2022/02/04/womens-workforce-participation-has-plummetedheres-how-to-reverse-the-trend-pandemic-labor-shortage-diversity-economy-tami-forman/ Accessed September 29, 2022.

there are ways to facilitate a successful return to work for women post-Covid: "flexibility and managerial support." The McKinsey report states:

> Women want to continue to work remotely after the pandemic, and they don't feel like remote work has caused them to miss out. Forty-five percent of women in financial services say they want to continue to work remotely, compared with 36 percent of men in finance. When it comes to the broader effect on their career of working remotely, both men and women in financial services generally agree on the extent to which their careers have stalled, lost ground, or advanced over the past year.[63]

Forty-five percent of women hoping to work remotely vs. 36 percent of men will be a significant change if firms don't accommodate women's needs and preferences in a post-COVID world.

Why do only women need "flexibility and managerial support"? That's a societal question we need to answer, but we're not going to be able to do that in this book.

Meanwhile, female leadership in big firms is now in real danger of *shrinking*, leaving even fewer mentors for young hires. It almost goes without saying that women with the largest salaries are most able to afford childcare and/or at-home help, but it's not that simple. They're also the ones who can afford some time out if that's their only option, and lots of people, like Jenny, are reassessing their life choices. It's also scary to see that once again

---

63 Ellingrud, Kweilin, Alexis Krivkovich, Marie-Claude Nadeau and Jill Zucker, "Closing the gender and race gaps in the North American financial industry." "https://www.mckinsey.com/industries/financial-services/our-insights/closing-the-gender-and-race-gaps-in-north-american-financial-services

women are shouldering the child-rearing burden, and we're talking about how to accommodate mothers with no consideration for how flexibility for fathers could help women continue making strides in their careers. Not to mention that all of these discussions and statistics are based on the experiences of heterosexual couples with kids and ignore other family structures.

We all had the opportunity to pause and reset during the first two years of the pandemic, and that's not a bad thing. But when there's this kind of dip in women participating at the top levels of corporate structure across America, it gives the "Old Boy Network" a bump that will be tough to level. And then, choices about work-life balance for women committed to the larger companies may no longer be theirs to make—unless they find a different path entirely, as I did.

Leaky Pipelines

We all know what leaky pipelines mean to the fossil fuel industry. Not good news. The same is true for the investment and banking industries.

Using the metaphor of the leaky pipeline to substitute for the corporate ladder's broken rung, imagine the cost to financial companies that do not promote women and minorities. The report from the House Committee on the Financial Services shares what they learned when studying the costs of failing to recruit and keep women and minorities: "Companies with diversity out-innovate and out-perform others. Employees of these companies are 45 percent more likely to report that their firm's market share grew over the previous year and 70 percent more likely to report that the firm captured a new market."[64]

It's a well-known fact that women and men complement each other in the workplace, both in terms of perspectives and skill sets, plus attitudes

64 "Diversity and Inclusion," op cit.

toward risk and collaboration. Hence, integrating more women into higher levels of financial companies would boost growth and income. The 2020 House Committee report found:

> Companies in the top-quartile for gender diversity on executive teams were 21% more likely to outperform on profitability. Companies in the top-quartile for ethnic/cultural diversity on executive teams were 33% more likely to have industry-leading profitability. That this relationship continues to be strong suggests that inclusion of highly diverse individuals—and the myriad ways in which diversity exists beyond gender (e.g., LGBTQ+, age/generation, international experience)—can be a key differentiator among companies.[65]

Knowing that, why don't companies embrace diversity?

Interestingly, some financial services company leaders are completely unaware of the real reasons for their leaky pipelines. Remember the story of my prior boss who kept replacing his dead exotic fish? The philosophy among people like that is: *One woman employee gone is easily replaceable by the next.* They probably feel that way about all employees—and in truth, we're all expendable—but it's harder to keep women employees for reasons leadership often doesn't understand. One lost female employee is one fewer woman in the pipeline, even if leadership has good intentions to promote.

The Wounds of Wall Street

In August 2022, Simon & Schuster published *Bully Market: My Story of Money and Misogyny at Goldman Sachs*, by Jamie Fiore Higgins, a woman who spent her entire career in finance at one Wall Street investment

65 Ibid.

bank. She was there for 18 years and did not get washed away by the leaky pipeline. In fact, she joined the company straight out of college and was making seven figures as a managing director when she left in 2016. She says that for a lot of that time, she had to check her morals at the 200 West Street revolving door—so much so that she felt the culture slowly corrupting her. The book is a riveting tell-all, mostly focused on what she calls the "sick Goldman culture" that eventually enveloped her. She writes: "I felt like human poison. I ruined everything I touched—marriages, careers, and relationships. After working for years in this awful environment, I'd become just as toxic as Goldman Sachs."[66]

Then there's Madeline Henry, Yale Class of 2014, who mined her experiences in a job she despised into a bestselling 2019 novel, *Breathe In, Cash Out.* Henry was recruited in her final year of college and "soon found herself an exhausted, overworked junior analyst (mind you, being paid in the top 0.1 person of all [Yale] graduates) but also somewhat miserable … Weeks are long, people are borderline nefarious, sleep deprivation and coffee addictions are applauded and a life outside of work is but a memory."[67] The heroine of her novel longs to leave a job at a top investment bank to become a yoga guru—complicated decision because she has "accidentally

66 Higgins, Jamie Fiore. *Bully Market: My Story of Money and Misogyny at Goldman Sachs.* NY: Simon and Schuster, 2022. Excerpt printed in "Goldman Sachs' Secrets Spill Out in New Book by Former Managing Director," Pam Martens and Russ Martens, *Wall Street Parade, August 29, 2022.* https://wallstreetonparade.com/2022/08/goldman-sachs-secrets-spill-out-in-new-book-by-a-former-managing-director/ Accessed September 26, 2022.
67 Lepore, Meredith. "This woman wrote a book about (and lived) every stressed-out Wall Street worker's career fantasy." "The Ladders," July 23, 2019. "https://www.theladders.com/career-advice/this-woman-wrote-a-book-about-and-lived-every-stressed-out-wall-street-workers-career-fantasy Accessed September 24, 2022.

slept with her boss and developed feelings for a coworker."[68] Are we finding a common thread here?

One friend of mine, Elise, who is a former Goldman Sachs employee, long ago shared with me her rather harrowing story. The firm recruited her while she was still completing her senior year at Harvard in the early 1990s. She interviewed and received an offer, which she was in the process of deciding whether to accept while she was in Florida for spring break. At one point, she looked up from her beach towel and saw her recruiter leering down at her. She immediately regretted having shared during the interview where she was headed on vacation.

Despite that unfortunate run-in, Elise took the job and arrived on Wall Street believing that this one guy was an aberration. He *couldn't* be representative of the entire department she was entering, could he? But it was only to find that "this one guy" was to be her supervisor. When she eventually stopped dodging his advances and outright rejected them, he froze her out, while remaining her supervisor and only assigning new work to other analysts.

Weeks later, the one deal Elise was still working on was with a partner notorious for his "work ethic." Late one Saturday afternoon, after a long week of sixteen-hour days, she realized she was sitting at her desk with nothing left to do. The partner, while still in his office, hadn't asked her for anything in over two hours. When she appeared at his door to ask if she could head home, he castigated her and shared that he had missed all his kids' birthday parties, and for that matter, their births, as well, because he had a real commitment to the firm. My friend recalls the level of exhaustion she felt at the time. Her (dry) mouth got ahead of her brain, she told

68 Ibid.

me, and she said, "Oh my gosh, I'm so sorry to hear that. I plan to be there when my children are born."

That remark sealed her fate; the following Monday, Elise had no projects at all, and after receiving no satisfactory suggestions from the human resources team, she threw up her hands and quit. When informing the managing director of her decision, she was told, "Not surprising. We didn't think you really fit our culture."

Of course, these examples come from one of the institutions in the finance world known for its reckless treatment of women employees. But they set the tone to which way too many firms aspire. In all venture capital and private equity firms, women constitute less than 10 percent of senior roles.[69]

How do these firms get away with this type of behavior? By wearing women down through constant abuse, such that they flee, and by forcing their employees to sign "non-defamation" agreements. Also, despite the fact that there are regulations about DEI, the laws have no teeth. In 2019, when the House Financial Services Committee conducted research for a major 2020 report on the state of diversity among the largest global banks and financial institutions, they didn't get as many responses to their surveys as would have been helpful. Among all the firms regulated by the FDIC, only 16.7 percent responded; of those regulated by the OCC, only 9.3 percent did. Section 342(3) of the Dodd-Frank Act requires the Office of Minority, Women, and Inclusion (OMWI) to submit annual reports to Congress on the actions financial services regulatory agencies and OMWI take regarding diversity policy and practices of regulated entities. But here's the rub:

69 Chandler, Sarah. "Why Are So Few Women in Finance? It's Complicated." Investopedia. February 25, 2022. https://www.investopedia.com/articles/investing/092315/why-are-so-few-women-finance-its-complicated.asp

the committee can ask for numbers, but there's no law requiring companies to provide them. Compliance is voluntary. Can you spell l-o-b-b-y-i-s-t-s?

Ye Olde Pipeline isn't newly broken. It's been leaking since it was built.

But what if we looked away from these big-name firms entirely? Perhaps the solution isn't to continue beating our heads against the brick walls surrounding these firms, but to get entrepreneurial and form innovative models. That's what I have chosen to do, and I'm not alone.

Oh, and by the way, who was that partner who drove Elise out of Goldman? She heard years later from the one friend she retained from that job that he never made it to age 50: unhealthy lifestyle, too much stress.

If Not on Wall Street, Then Where Are We?

There's really no way you'd know about all the women forging ahead in the new investment world. As I've said, the media doesn't focus on us. But we exist.

In Chapter One, I introduced you to Sallie Krawcheck in my explanation of robo-investing. Krawcheck is the woman who led Merrill Lynch Wealth Management and Smith Barney and was CFO then CEO of Citigroup/Citi Wealth Management, and after years of being discounted by the men at the companies she now *led,* she made it her life's mission to help women take control of their financial futures. She founded Ellevest, which, as I shared, you can download as an app. (Maybe you already have, and I should let Sallie know I deserve a referral fee.) If you haven't, I'll review: You can invest super easily via the app; you can set up automatic deposits to a stock fund and/or a retirement fund; there are no minimums; and, you get quick personal customer service even if you have just pennies in your account. What I didn't mention at that point is that Ellevest also offers seminars that help women understand what they and their money are doing. That's key.

Ellevest is a brilliant innovation, and as usual, Krawcheck has been a leader. Ellevest burst onto the scene with this new approach geared toward women, and now, not only has she helped women start investing with greater comfort and confidence, but she has also opened the door for more women entrepreneurs to add updates to her model—twists that have multi-generational and gender-non-specific appeal.

Eve Halimi and Anam Lakhani developed an idea while at Columbia University that they've taken beyond campus: Alinea Invest. Their motivation stemmed from their own frustration navigating financial markets. They get it: they explain it's not some failing on our part; it's just that unless we have parents who are investor savvy—in my case, my mother—we aren't taught how to manage money.

Alinea has been community-driven from the start, Halimi and Lakhani say. It's as if they've birthed a modern, inclusive version of the Old Boy Network that's even a step above the (Stanford-founded) Robinhood, with its welcoming feel and mentoring modules geared to the financial world newbie. Halimi and Lakhani recognized when founding Alinea that there was a staunch discrepancy among their college peers: some leaned into investing, and others shied away because they felt it wasn't for them. But those who didn't engage only felt disinclined because they didn't know enough. Alinea offers the comforts of simplicity, no minimums, learning along the way, and a sharing aspect akin to that on Spotify, which leads to constant discovery of new opportunities.

Alinea's technology takes the Ellevest and Robinhood breakthroughs to another level. To understand what they're all about, it helps to think of analogous apps in other categories. For example, the insanely popular Calm was the first app to offer daily meditations, soothing sounds, and sleep therapy listening. But the recent startup Aura goes another step, tailoring listening and viewing to the individual: no one-size-fits-all meditations or therapeutic listening. Aura's founders built in an algorithm that sends you material based on what you "liked" the day before. (Yes, it's like Facebook's, only without the evil.) As seen on "the other meditation app," InsightTimer, you can also find coaches you like and follow them or work with them live.

On Alinea, like on Aura and the universally relied-upon music app Spotify, you complete a quiz after downloading so your choices are personalized from the start. Alinea even has "investment baskets" that are like playlists on Spotify, which you can share with other users. Say you're interested only in women-owned, socially responsible, or green companies. That's what you'll see, and that's what your followers will find, too. Again, no minimums, lots of support tailored to those who have felt excluded from the Wall Street universe, with learning and mega-community.

And if you're not leaning toward an app, there is an explosion of diverse entrepreneurial mentors to suit each and every one of us. You've probably heard of Michelle Singletary, who writes the nationally syndicated personal finance column "The Color of Money." She had her own television show and routinely appears on NPR, national talk shows, television networks, and cable giants. Singletary founded a ministry in which men and women volunteer to help others with financial challenges, and she and her husband teach financial literacy to prison inmates. Tonya Rapley founded My Fab Finance. She's a domestic violence survivor who calls herself a "citizen of the world" in that she is an American citizen who was born in the

Philippines. Her company was named the "New Face of Wealth Building" by *Black Enterprise* magazine. These women not only stride ahead, they also give back. I get that; it's one of my missions, too.

The world from which women are excluded continues on, with places like Goldman still bullying the rest. However, younger generations of women are seeking entry into the markets, demanding better services that include education and community-building, and choosing ESG (Environmental Social and Governance) stocks. There's no more time for whining. We need to grab the bull by the horns (pardon the market pun) and ride like a cowgirl.

Not a Texan, like me? The tide is turning, and we're cresting the wave.

$

CHAPTER SEVEN

All the Powerful Women You've Never Heard Of

"There are so many inspirational women out there," begins Dana Michelle Cook in the trailer for the 2014 film *The Empowerment Project,* a documentary about the exceptional qualities and achievements of ordinary American women. "But why is it so hard to see them?" Cook asks.[70]

Along with *Empowerment Project* co-founder Sarah Moshman, Cook and other filmmakers traveled cross-country for thirty days obtaining footage for the documentary, driven by the innate knowledge that "powerful, inspiring women were all around us, but we weren't seeing them in the media." They decided to change that with this project. Their goal was "to encourage, empower, and inspire the next generation of strong women to go after their career ambitions."[71]

The film features seventeen positive and powerful women leaders across a variety of lifestyles and industries, including a pilot, an astronaut,

70 https://www.youtube.com/watch?v=UK_-d9N8KzE. Accessed 11/10/2022.
71 www.empowermentproject.com Accessed 11/10/2022.

a mathematician, and a Navy admiral, plus many more. It challenges the audience to ask themselves, "What would you do if you weren't afraid to fail?"

Why *are* we so afraid of failing? Could it be that we hold ourselves to higher standards higher than men do? Because we've had to? And that we're more vulnerable to criticism if we fail? Or could it be that we just haven't seen enough of our sisters succeed?

Karen Lynch

In 2022, CVS Health CEO Karen Lynch ranked No. 1 on *Fortune's* Most Powerful Women list for the second year in a row.[72] Lynch is, indeed, a rock star.

Under Lynch's guidance, the company generated $292 billion in revenue in 2021, a nine percent jump over the previous year, and profits climbed 10 percent to nearly $8 billion. In addition, in the year after Lynch took the helm, CVS shares skyrocketed 42 percent, outpacing the S&P 500's two percent rise. The company did a masterful job administering COVID-19 vaccines and continues to aspire to be "America's one-stop health shop." Lynch also made *Fortune's* Change the World list in 2022 due to her focus on customers' mental health and her implementation of a program to reduce suicide attempts.[73]

Lynch also has a remarkable personal story. She was raised by a single mother until she was twelve, at which point she lost her mother to suicide—hence her strong interest in *mental* health. She and her three siblings

72 "The 50 Most Powerful Women in Business." *Fortune.* https://fortune.com/most-powerful-women/ Accessed 11/10/2022.

73 Fortune's Change the World List. https://fortune.com/change-the-world/ Accessed 11/10/2022.

were then cared for by an aunt who died of cancer when Lynch was in her early 20s—hence her dedication to *physical* health.[74] These are hurdles that could knock anyone on her ass. The humble Lynch's story is one of extraordinary determination and courage.

So why hasn't Lynch been widely covered by the media? Why must we be inundated daily with stories about Elon Musk and not heroes like Lynch, who have risen from early challenges to make huge positive changes in the world? *Why isn't* she *opening for SNL?* Aside from the fact that she probably doesn't want to, the media hasn't anointed her as a household name.

Sure, you say, at least that way she's not a *joke* or someone everyone loves to hate, like the holy bro trinity of Musk, Zuckerberg, and Bezos. Perhaps the problem is that women who work hard for success are too busy to care about their social media profiles. You have to look for them on LinkedIn, and let's be serious, you're only there to do some serious professional networking.

But if I were to list highly successful male CEOs who are not the equivalent of James Bond villains, my bet is that you'd still recognize their names, whereas if I list women who have broken through that C-suite glass ceiling, you'd say, "Who, again?"

Let's play. Can you name the company?

1. Warren Buffett
2. Jamie Dimon

---

74 Lynch, Karen and Forbes Staff."How One of the Most Powerful People in Healthcare Turned Tragedy into her Driving Passion." *Forbes.com*. April 24, 2018. https://www.forbes.com/sites/forbes-summit-talks/2018/04/24/how-personal-tragedy-drives-the-passion-behind-one-of-healthcares-most-powerful-women/ Accessed 11/10/2022.

3. Steve Jobs
4. Tim Cook
5. Jack Welch
6. Lloyd Blankfein
7. Sam Walton
8. Bill Gates
9. Larry Page
10. Dara Khosrowshahi

Now, can you identify the companies these women have led or are currently leading?

1. Mary Barra
2. Susan Wojcicki
3. Safra Ada Catz
4. Meg Whitman
5. Mary Sammon
6. Jane Fraser
7. Carol Tomé
8. Judith McKenna
9. Abigail Johnson
10. Heywood Donegan

(You can find the answers at the end of this chapter.)

There are so many amazing sagas of women's business success you've never heard of. Yes, the media fails to showcase us, although they don't hesitate a second to point out when one of us fails. And often, we women are called in when the going is rough, almost as if to set us up in case the problems are too overwhelming or deep-seated to solve. *Almost as if.*

But first, some examples of women who have defied all odds.

Rosalind Brewer

Rosalind Brewer became the first Black woman to lead one of CVS's major competitors, Walgreens Boots Alliance, as CEO in March 2021. Being the first wasn't something she aspired to, she said in October 2022 at Fortune's Most Powerful Women Summit. "I'm still walking in and being the only [Black woman] in the room," she said, adding that diversity in corporate America falls far behind stated goals. Before Walgreens, she was the first Black American and first woman to become the COO and group president at Starbucks. In 2022, Brewer was one of only two Black women leading Fortune 500 companies—the other was Thasunda Brown Duckett, CEO of the financial organization TIAA. The youngest of five children, Brewer was also the first in her family to attend college. She shared at the summit that she never knew how many skills she had and never imagined she'd be leading a Fortune 500 company.[75] Brewer overcame that thinking, which persists for women in the business world despite endless empowerment workshops and self-affirmations. And it's worse for women of color.

As TIAA's CEO, Duckett leads a company whose mission is defined by financial inclusion and opportunity. Duckett joined TIAA in 2021 after serving as CEO of Chase Consumer Banking, where she oversaw a banking network with more than $600 billion in deposits and 50,000 employees. Before that, she was CEO of Chase Auto Finance. Duckett says her

75 "2021 Forbes Power Women's Summit: The Visionary: Transforming A New Tomorrow." Forbes.com Dec. 21, 2021. https://www.forbes.com/video/6286638010001/2021-forbes-power-womens-summit-the-visionary-transforming-a-new-tomorrow/?sh=6650515a750c Accessed 11/10/2022.

personal commitment to helping ensure retirees get to truly enjoy their golden years stems from the experiences of her father, Otis Brown, who never took advantage of his own company's retirement plan beyond his pension. "The information his company was providing [about retirement benefits] didn't connect with a man in the warehouse," she says. Because her father's experience meant he missed out on years of savings and interest, Duckett said, she reminds organizations to ensure that they communicate with all their employees about how to save for retirement—including reaching out to security guards and admins, not just executives.

Then there is Eileen McDonnell, CEO of the insurance firm Penn Mutual (a Fortune 1000 company). She was single and in her mid-40s when she adopted a daughter from Russia—*before* she had the top job. She had actually stepped away from corporate life to work as a consultant so she could have more time as a parent, but the then-CEO of Penn Mutual approached her for the role of CMO. She told the board she would need to be guaranteed flexibility because she didn't want to be looked down upon for stepping out to be a reader in her daughter's classroom, for example. Two years later, she was promoted to president and became CEO in 2012.[76]

These women's motivations are profound.

Lynch explains that her early life drove her into health care, where she could make a serious difference, and Brewer, her counterpart at Walgreens, has a similar answer. Both women assumed CEO status during the pandemic. Brewer has said that during the early part of COVID-19, she experienced, through friends and family, how many health inequities

---

76 "TIAA CEO Thasunda Brown Duckett's father missed out on years of retirement savings. She wants to make sure yours doesn't." *Fortune.com* October 11, 2022. https://fortune.com/2022/10/11/tiaa-ceo-thasunda-brown-duckett-retirement-savings-mpw-summit/ Accessed 11/10/2022.

existed. She had run pharmacies at both Walmart and Sam's Club earlier in her career. She says that she decided to take everything she'd learned and use it to help people struggling with one of the biggest problems they'd ever face; rather than being deterred by the crisis, she was motivated by it, and she says taking the lead in a crisis is one of the fastest ways to see how an industry and a company need to adapt to new challenges.

Cathy Hughes

Another woman of color, Cathy Hughes, is founder and chairperson of Urban One, formerly known as Radio One, and the largest African American owned and operated broadcast in the US. Hughes had a son when she was sixteen years old, was divorced, and raising him on her own by the time she became the first Black woman to own a radio station ranked No. 1 in *any* major market.

Hughes credits being a young single mom with inspiring her to become an entrepreneur. She tells a story of heading home to take care of her son when he was ill and being told by her employer not to come back if she walked out that door. That was it for her—she wanted control over her professional life, and she was determined to get it. She believed professional autonomy was the only way she would be able to be there for her son the way she wanted to be.[77]

Mellody Hobson

Have you ever heard of Mellody Hobson? Recently, I read a blurb about her that said she became nationally known in 2013 after marrying *Star Wars* filmmaker George Lucas. But what had she done up until then?

77 Harris, Janelle. "So What Do You Do, Cathy Hughes?" *Media Bistro.com* https://www.mediabistro.com/interviews/so-what-do-you-do-cathy-hughes-founder-of-tv-one-and-radio-one/ Accessed 11/10/2022.

Hobson was the youngest of six children born and raised by a single mom. When she was little, her mother knew so little about money management that the family was often evicted, or their phone would get disconnected, or the lights would be turned off. She decided that she wanted to understand money because if she understood it, she would know how to be free.

Hobson found her own orthodontist when she was ten years old and got a payment plan from him for the $2,500 treatment; she paid about $50 per month. From the age of five, she would hand her mom's money to the cashier at McDonald's or the grocery store. From there, she learned how to count change, compute tips, and write out checks that her mom would sign. She borrowed money to go to Princeton, and when she graduated and bought her first mattress, she calculated the per-diem cost and didn't feel as bad about the expense. She lived off her starting salary at Ariel Investments, the first Black-owned financial management and mutual fund companies in the US, in 2021, managing nearly $13 billion in assets, and paid off her student debt while saving up for an apartment. Now, she serves as the company's co-CEO and president.

Hobson contributed financial segments to *Good Morning America* for many years and is a regular contributor on financial issues on *CBS This Morning*. She's on the board of many organizations, including JPMorgan Chase & Co., the Chicago Public Education Fund, the Lucas Museum of Narrative Art, and the Sundance Institute. She was the first Black woman to lead the Chicago Economics Club. She's also chairman of the board of Starbucks. Her family foundation recently donated funds to build residential housing on the site of the former Wilson College at Princeton; the Wilson name was removed from Princeton due to Woodrow Wilson's history as a segregationist. The new residential college will bear Hobson's name.[78]

But Hobson became famous when she married George Lucas in 2013?

Jennifer Piepszak will be co-CEO of the consumer division of JPMorgan Chase in 2022, the arm that oversees card services, home lending, consumer and community banking, and auto financing. The consumer banking division in banking is often the one in which women have greater success advancing than many others, such as the investment banking segment, where Piepszak started. At JPMorgan Chase, the consumer banking division has more than 130,000 employees and serves more than 60 million households and four million small businesses in the US Barron's named Piepszak one of the 100 Most Influential Women in US. Finance, and in 2019, Crain's named her the second-most powerful woman in New York. The word on the financial street is that she is the top candidate to replace Jamie Dimon as CEO when he retires. We need to know her name.

Okay, so there are plenty of high-achieving businesswomen out there, *even in finance.* But what happens when one stumbles? It seems the higher the woman's achievement, when she makes a misstep—no matter how minor—the more enthusiastically the media devours her for lunch. And we take it. It's weird, as if one of the spiked heels broke off our uncomfortable pumps, so we just stopped walking altogether.

Worse, sometimes we even join in on the feeding frenzy.

78 Marsh, Ariana. "Mellody Hobson On the Importance of Achieving Financial Freedom and Investing in Yourself." *Harpersbazaar.com* June 29, 2021. https://www.harpersbazaar.com/culture/features/a36831755/mellody-hobson-june-july-2021/ Accessed 11/10/2022.

It's even easier to name high-profile women the media loves to hate than it is to pair up successful female CEOs with their companies. Let's start with politics. Nancy Pelosi and Liz Cheney come to mind. I bet you could name a dozen more in seconds. Just think of any high-profile woman who isn't afraid to say what she really thinks—women who stand up for what they believe in no matter the cost. They might as well be wearing bull's eyes on their backs.

One perfect example of a highly accomplished businesswoman who just couldn't win is Carly Fiorina. As chairman of technology, president, and then CEO of Hewlett-Packard, she was the first woman to hold all three titles at a tech company, and as CEO, she was the top-ranking businesswoman in the US. At first, she received positive media coverage—for breaking the glass ceiling, yes, but even more so for her good looks and style. After her appearances at the Academy Awards, the opening of Disney World's Mission: Space, and the World Economic Forum in Davos, Switzerland, she was lauded as "a Hollywood-class icon" by one of the male members of the HP board. After she was fired, though, Fiorina was demonized as someone who sought too much attention in the media and didn't spend enough time in the corner office. And as a candidate for the Republican nomination for president, she fell victim to harassment from Donald J. Trump. To be fair, Trump is perhaps the #1 openly sexist figure America has ever sent to the national stage, blithely making points among his base by launching insults at all his opponents with a particularly misogynist approach toward women. In an interview with *Rolling Stone* in 2016, he was quoted as saying about Fiorina, "Look at that face. Would anyone vote for that?" The interviewer didn't challenge him—which is itself problematic and an example of how ingrained misogyny and sexism are in our culture, but I digress.[79] Apparently, in American media, women's looks are fair game, even when we're talking about women with extraordinary track records in leadership. Or maybe especially so.

Cathie Wood is a more recent example of the same. She started life in a modest family; her parents were immigrants from Ireland, and her dad served in the US Air Force. At the University of Southern California, she majored in finance and economics and graduated with a *summa cum laude*. Her first job after college was as an assistant economist; she continued as an analyst and portfolio manager, co-founded a hedge fund, then in 2001 went to work for AllianceBernstein as chief investment officer of global thematic strategies, where she managed $5 billion for twelve years. She founded Ark Invest in 2014 after AllianceBernstein deemed her idea for managing funds based on "disruptive innovation" too risky. In 2020, *Bloomberg* editor-in-chief at the time Matthew Winkler named Wood the best stock picker of the year, and by March 2021, two of the funds she was running were on the list of the ten largest female-run funds based on total net assets.

Wood went on to become a cult hero in 2021 for young investors. Then, 2022 proved to be a painful reality check for her and her devotees. Wood's flagship fund, the ARK Innovation ETF, had risen 157 percent in 2020 despite the market turbulence brought on by COVID-19. She had large holdings in Zoom, Roku, and Teladoc Health—also known as "stay-at-home" stocks. Also, she was an early devotee of Elon Musk and Tesla, which surged in 2020. She became known as a sort of "disruptive innovation evangelist," and investors poured money into her fund.

79 Lopez, German. "Donald Trump on Carly Fiorina: 'Look at that Face.'" Vox.com September 9, 2015. https://www.vox.com/2015/9/10/9302321/donald-trump-carly-fiorina Accessed 11/10/2022.

However, when the tide turned on the stay-at-homes, which were expected to dip once the world reopened, ARK sank like a stone, losing 23 percent in 2021, while the S&P roared back and gained 27 percent. In 2022, ARK was doing no better; by November, the ARK Innovation ETF's value had shrunk by 60 percent from its meteoric high point and new low point, plunging at a much more precipitous rate than the 2022 S&P. The firm's assets under management in all of its ETFs declined from more than $60 billion in February 2021 to $16 billion at the end of the first quarter of 2022.[80] Wood dropped off *Forbes*' list of America's richest self-made women. Those who invested in her fund in 2020 had gone full circle, watching their investments peak and then sink back to where they started—only now, adjusted for inflation, they were worth less.

Wood was then excoriated in the media as her critics took *schadenfreude* to a whole new level. Perhaps it was inevitable that someone so sure of her predictions and so rewarded by the markets early on would generate the kind of envy that can so easily turn to derision. But her excitement about "disruptive innovation" didn't come from nowhere. The phenomenon was named by Clay Christensen of Harvard Business School all the way back in 1995 and was called by many, including Wall Street analysts and academics, the most influential business idea of the early Twenty-First Century. The term describes a process by which a project or service takes root in simple applications at the bottom of a market—like Zoom, inexpensive and accessible—and then relentlessly moves upmarket, eventually displacing established competitors.

80 Tucker, Hank. "Ark Invest CEO Cathie Wood's Net Worth Slashed By 65% As Tech Bets Sour In 2022." *Forbes.com* June 14, 2022. https://www.forbes.com/sites/hanktucker/2022/06/14/ark-invest-ceo-cathie-woods-tesla-zoom-coinbase-net-worth-slashed-by-65-as-tech-bets-sour-in-2022/?sh=18a104c5539c Accessed 11/10/2022.

Humility, never a bad characteristic, might have served Wood better when her funds were soaring. She celebrated her success in 2021 in part by mocking old-school investors who were naysayers when she launched ARK Innovation ETF, and the lesson is clear: those people don't take well to being chided, and they don't sit idly by if you crater. They hit back hard, in this case by structuring ways to make money off her downfall, by shorting her fund. In 2022, others made millions off betting against her.

As widely reported, those who recognized early 2021 as a bubble also knew that Wood brazenly went big into Tesla and Bitcoin and told off the people who advised her to be more cautious. Even those not shorting her were lying in wait to tell the media that her approach was "perilous" and even that she was part of the bear market's problem. When she continued as a contrarian and poured more capital into the fund, the rating company Morningstar, which usually remains dispassionate, published a harsh critique of Wood and downgraded ARK to negative. In April 2022, Morningstar analysts used vocabulary like "wretched performance," "poor risk management," and "inability to navigate challenging territory." [81]

Her self-congratulatory glory in the payoffs for her 2020 risk taking was nothing compared to the scolding she took in 2022.

By mid-2022, Wood acknowledged that a global recession was threatening, but she remained relentlessly optimistic, taking a long-term view. But her reputation was so beaten up that her positive attitude began to look fake. The voices of those who believe she's onto something have been so drowned out by those eager to discredit her that it remained to be seen whether she could recover. She was fighting three battles: one with

81 "Morningstar Downgrades Cathie Woods' Flagship Fund." *Financial Advisors Magazine.* April 1, 2022. https://www.fa-mag.com/news/morningstar-downgrades-cathie-wood-s-ark-flagship-fund Accessed 11/10/2022.

the global markets, one with those profiting by betting against her, and the third with triumphant haters.

When men become outspoken contrarians in the business and finance world, they become media darlings: innovators, forward-thinkers, trendsetters. They can even get elected president, despite tanking multiple companies, failing to pay their bills, and violating a slew of laws. When respectable people like Warren Buffett blunder, people chalk it up to that old saying that no one is right 100 percent of the time. When Wood was brave enough to buck the trends, she was called a "capital evaporator," toxic to the market itself. Meanwhile, Wood, ARK employees, and a vast number of investors have stayed with her, and as of this writing, it's hard to predict who will have the last laugh.

At least, as Hillary Clinton might quip, no one was talking about her hairstyle, pantsuits, or weight.

In 2018, there was surprising news about the NYSE. For the first time since the group was established in 1792, it was to be led by a woman, Stacy Cunningham.

At the time, Cunningham told NPR interviewer Lulu Garcia-Navarro that she didn't think gender had anything to do with her being selected and that she didn't consider her gender a huge factor when it came to pursuing opportunities that led her to break into the top ranks of the finance industry. Instead, she said, it was thanks to trailblazers who came before her, women who entered the financial space long before the idea of a woman CEO at the NYSE seemed possible. She stressed that younger generations should push gender boundaries because it helps the next generation.[82]

82 Garciz-Navarro, Lulu. "It was never about my gender." *NPR.org.* June 10, 2018. https://www.npr.org/2018/06/10/618271798/it-was-never-about-my-gender-nyse-s-first-female-president-thanks-her-trailblaze Accessed 11/10/2022.

In December 2021, Intercontinental Exchange (ICE), the parent company of the NYSE, released new surprising information: Cunningham was suddenly stepping down amid a shakeup of top management. Meanwhile, ICE's founder, chairman, and CEO, Jeffrey Sprecher, quietly disclosed that he was leaving his role as chairman of the NYSE. The press release didn't explain what prompted the changes. However, Sprecher noted that ICE's past performance set a high bar for the new management team. Plus, news had just broken that the NYSE was losing out on IPO revenues to Nasdaq for the third year in a row—the same amount of time that Cunningham oversaw the NYSE. Under Cunningham, the NYSE entered a completely new era through necessary updates to technology that made it possible to migrate to an exclusively electronic environment during COVID-19 and the unprecedented shuttering of the trading floor.[83]

Replacing Cunningham was the second woman in the position, Lynn Martin, who has said she believes success depends on two aspects of management: collaboration and innovation. A fanatical problem solver, she grew up learning to code on a Commodore 64 computer. These days, she defies the notion that you have to be on site 24/7 to be a good leader: she gets her creative ideas while at indoor cycling classes—sometimes two forty-five-minute classes in a row.[84]

Perhaps Martin is talking about what another female CEO, Evelyn Webster, refers to as "the magic of Soul Cycle."

---

83 "Stacy Cunningham, First Female NYSE President, To Step Down." *WSJ.com.* https://www.wsj.com/articles/stacey-cunningham-first-female-nyse-president-to-step-down-11638817680. Accessed 11/10/2022.

84 Cramer, Farrell. "New NYSE President Lynn Martin Brings Tech Background to the Big Board." December 6, 2021. https://www.nyse.com/taking-stock/lynn-martin-brings-tech-background-to-the-big-board Accessed 11/10/2022.

Soul Cycle, Equinox's sister company that offers steeply priced, pay-as-you-go indoor cycling in darkened, candle-lit studios pumping loud music, needed quite a bit of creativity to solve the multitude of problems it was facing at the end of the lockdown phase of COVID-19. It was reeling from accusations that instructors fat shamed and used racist, homophobic, and ethnic slurs; struggling with deficits and closures due to long-term pandemic closures; challenged by Peloton and the at-home exercise culture; extricating themselves from the culture wars (left-leaning patrons boycotted after learning that the majority shareholder of the parent company sponsored political fundraisers for Trump); and recovering from the sudden departure of prior CEO Melanie Whelan.

Whelan had become a bit of a "women in leadership" guru herself over her time with this company, which thrives on a devoted client base. When she was leading SoulCycle, her advice to other women was to have a really clear voice and to speak strongly in order to avoid being devalued by louder voices at the table.[85] The new CEO, Evelyn Webster, who took over in December of 2020 while all hell was breaking loose, has a murkier but somehow understandable notion of how we can reach our goals. She describes the shared as "the secret sauce" that makes the brand succeed as shared experience.[86]

The unique aspects of the Soul Cycle environment are meant to unleash the physical, mental, emotional, and spiritual simultaneously.

85 Bryant, Adam. "SoulCycle CEO on her college wake-up call and the No. 1 thing women can do to get ahead." *CNBC.com* May 14, 2018. https://www.cnbc.com/2018/05/14/soulcycle-ceo-melanie-whelan-the-no-1-thing-women-can-do-to-succeed.html Accessed 11/10/2022.

86 Rella, Emily. "For SoulCycle CEO Evelyn Webster, the Way Forward is Through Accountability, Inclusivity and Purpose." July 1, 2021. https://www.entrepreneur.com/leadership/for-soulcycle-ceo-evelyn-webster-the-way-forward-is/376226 Accessed 11/10/2022.

Whether a believer or not, the interesting aspect within the context of leadership is *community.* SoulCycle class participants experience something unusual together, and there is nothing more atypical (and sometimes lonely) than being a woman business leader, especially in finance.

We don't have to climb on stationary bikes (unless we feel like it). But if we don't find a way to promote one another's achievements and downplay the sexist media's grueling dissection of everything about us, from the way we dress to our body shape and size to our very human inability to be right 100 percent of the time, we've basically lost this game.

We have to pay attention to each other. We need to learn each other's names. We have to patronize one another's businesses, hire one another, and support each other through tough times. We need to invest in each other's companies. And we need to pay it forward by mentoring younger women who are looking to us to help open up the doors that we had to bang our fists on.

We are out there, and we need to be sure everyone knows that.

Answers to the quiz:

Male CEOs:

1. *Warren Buffett: Berkshire Hathaway*
2. *Jamie Dimon: JP Morgan Chase*
3. *Steve Jobs: Apple*
4. *Tim Cook: Apple*
5. *Jack Welch: IBM*
6. *Lloyd Blankfein: Goldman, Sachs*
7. *Sam Walton: Walmart*

8. *Bill Gates: Microsoft*
9. *Larry Page: Google*
10. *Dara Khosrowshahi: Uber*

Female CEOs:

1. *Mary Barra: General Motors*
2. *Susan Wojcicki: YouTube*
3. *Safra Ada Catz: Oracle*
4. *Meg Whitman: Hewlett-Packard*
5. *Mary Sammon: Rite Aid Corp.*
6. *Jane Fraser: CitiGroup*
7. *Carol Tomé: UPS*
8. *Judith McKenna: Walmart International*
9. *Abigail Johnson: Fidelity*
10. *Heywood Donegan: Rite Aid Corp.*

$

CHAPTER EIGHT

What's Your Pain Threshold?

Women have an incredibly high tolerance for pain.

I'm writing this book in 2022, the year US Supreme Court Justice Samuel Alito wrote the Dobbs decision, which reversed forty-nine years of American women's right to choose whether to carry a pregnancy to term.

Among the women I know where I live—Texas—opinions about abortion vary widely, and it's definitely not a topic you want to bring up over drinks. However, we all agree on one thing: It makes no sense that men make the rules that women must follow. That's particularly true right now here in Texas, where even supporting a woman's tough decision to terminate a pregnancy can now be considered illegal. In my state, pro-life activists or just nosy neighbors are now free to spy on women and their friends and family and report anything suspicious. The Texas state legislature that passed this bill is 75 percent male; the governor who signed it is, too.

Remarkably, in 2022, as I write this book, male US Supreme Court Justices will outnumber the female justices by one; the ratio will be five men to four women. We have had 116 Supreme Court justices since the nation's founding, and only six of them have been women. We're actually living in enlightened times.

But several of my friends enjoyed pointing out that if men were the ones who got pregnant and delivered babies, the human species probably would have gone extinct millions of years ago. One said, "How many pregnancies do you think Samuel Alito has brought to term?"

You have to admit, that's not only funny; it's also damn real.

Have you ever noticed that there are some pretty popular books and films out there that celebrate women's ability to bear pain? And even enjoy it?

Again, no judgment on whatever kinky thing you choose to do in your bedroom (or kitchen, or other type of room), but ahem, *Fifty Shades of Grey* has sold about 200 million copies worldwide. The box office total for the films? Way more than a billion dollars.

All right, another complicated topic. But get this: There are indie films that also hit it big and to high acclaim that celebrate women's ability to bear pain without any fun involved.

There's the 2012 film *Would You Rather* which is a creepy twist on the somewhat adolescent parlor game of the same name. In it, a philanthropist offers to pay the cancer treatment expenses of the main character Iris's brother. He'll even get her brother on the short list for a bone marrow treatment. One hitch. She has to survive his own version of the game. One dinner in, and she already knows it's twisted, but it's too late. Anyone who decides to ditch gets shot. Wheel in the shock machine. What follows includes knives, whips, ice picks, waterboarding, tooth extractions, etc. If you are going to watch this charming film, skip ahead because I'm about to give you a spoiler.

Iris wins, but when she gets home, her brother has already committed suicide, so he is no longer a burden to the family.

Wait! There's another, more recent version of the "women can survive anything" movie: *The Odds*, which came out in 2018. In this peach of a psychological thriller (the gore is off-stage, so it doesn't qualify as horror), a young woman joins an underground game of pain endurance, hoping to win the prize of $1 million. She too needs the money—in this case to help support her daughter, because all her previous bad decisions have made her incapable of doing so any other way. She signs on to endure rounds of torture involving increasing levels of pain as her opponent engages in ever-more horrific methods to manipulate and defeat her, while wealthy patrons observe it all through webcams and bet on which of the twenty contestants will win. Turns out the only character she thinks is helping her, the "Game Master," is the guy designing the torture—your basic psychopath. This indie flick was nominated for multiple awards, mainly based on the performance of Abbi Butler, the actress who plays the nameless main character. It's all about her ability to show simultaneous pain and stamina.

There are many more, but I'm sure you've already caught the thread: a woman needs money for altruistic reasons, has to survive torture to get it.

Sounds like fifty years of marriage to the wrong rich guy. *And are there any right rich guys if you're depending on them to be secure?*

Even writing all this is starting to feel like torture, and I apologize if reading it is. But I want you to remember the point: We *so* do not have to live that way. No matter what we never learned when we were younger, no matter what mistakes we have made, we can take charge long before the real torture begins.

And to me, the torture begins with missed opportunities.

You've learned in this book that you can take control of your finances—first by learning the basics, which you can learn the nitty gritty about in plenty of other places, but which include managing your spending and debt in such a way that you will have something to invest. You've learned you can start small, investing at least a modest percentage of your income, and maybe even with a robo-investor app like Ellevest: Nothing fancy necessary, and preferably one founded by a woman and designed to help women improve their—our—financial literacy.

You've learned that most men in the financial industry ignore us. You've learned about the big finance companies and that most, if not all, financial advisors do not have your best interests at heart for reasons built right into the system. You've learned that financial institutions are actually missing out by not working more with women because as it turns out women investors do better than men long-term. We are more patient, we research more; and IMHO, we're smarter and more ethical. (Shh, don't mention that to your decent guy friends and lovers.) We certainly have better reasons for socking that money away and watching it grow. How many women do you know who have a mid-life crisis that leads them to blow a huge pile of money buying a Porsche they can't afford?

And most importantly, you've learned that there is an entire world of investments out there that are not in the stock market. That you can understand it and benefit from it.

First, one last review of what and whom to avoid as you go about it.

Women fronting men

There are quite a few hedge funds out there these days, led by women. Be careful. Smart Wall Street boys have discovered that we're looking for companies run by women because a) we trust them more and b) they'll pitch the bitch in the first place. But a lot of these firms are actually run by the men on their boards, or the male-run mega-financial institutions that back them with male CEOs and boards. Put simply, it's places like Goldman Sachs trying to capture more women's money. And they're super savvy with marketing and public relations.

In 2021, Goldman announced the "Launch with GS" initiative, a huge investment in what they called a "Female Founders Fund" (FFF). Note the word "Goldman" doesn't appear in the initiative name; you could easily mistake GS for Girl Scouts. Anyway, the FFF is an "early-stage fund investing in the next generation of transformational technology companies founded by women." Sounds oh-so-good, right? It gets even better as they explain what the FFF does: It's a seed stage fund that invests exclusively in female-founded companies. "It has invested in more than 50 companies across B2B, Consumer, Fintech and Healthcare industries, 70% of which are led by BIPOC founders." Wow, you say. When Goldman invested, the FFF had funds of more than $90 million. Read on:

> With Fund III, FFF has created the largest fund for seed capital specifically for female founders. The fund will continue to invest in innovative platforms and products that support diverse communities, including LGBTQ+, women of color, parents and beyond. In addition to investing, the firm is committed to counseling founders throughout their journeys with the help of their

> ecosystem of more than 50,000 female founders and investors … "Goldman Sachs is proud to invest in FFF, as we also strongly believe that female-founded businesses generate strong returns," said Suzanne Gauron, head of *Launch With GS*. "Less than 3% of US venture capital goes to all women founding teams and Fund III represents a key opportunity to level the playing field."[87]

They put it right in the press release! "Fund III represents a key opportunity to level the playing field" could be read as "here's a chance to increase early investment in women-owned enterprises." Or it could mean that we just bought into FFF at such a huge level that we have leveled the playing field back to where only the top (male) players are the referees.

I don't want to suggest that FFF sold out; indeed, they've done well to attract all those millions and will be able to direct them to women-led companies. But once Goldman is involved, you can be sure there will be more female-headed companies with male boards.

Women, BIPOC, and LGBTQ+ employees are often hired so companies can apply for federal funding that demands diversity. There are endless stories about being the only Black person in the C-suite at an organization (and how tricky negotiating that can be). Now, women, BIPOC, and LGBTQ+ may be in title roles to attract women and/or socially responsible investors while men are still behind the curtain like the Wizard of Oz. You can't make this shit up. Or at least, you don't have to.

---

87 "Goldman Sachs' *Launch with GF* Initiative Announces Investment in Female Founders Fund. July 23, 2021. https://www.goldmansachs.com/media-relations/press-releases/2021/launch-with-gs-investment-in-female-founders-fund.html Accessed November 29, 2022.

So exercise caution. Be sure the place you're putting your money is where you really want it to be.

Which brings us to …

Buyer beware

So you've taken my advice, and you're ready to invest in private equity (PE). Remember, investing in any PE fund can be risky—it's important to know the quality of the information you're getting. In many, many cases, the owner of the fund may watch all his deals fall apart, only to continue to collect big fees from investors. The controversy surrounding private equity is that whatever happens to the company acquired, private equity makes money anyway if the owner of the fund is not a fiduciary, like I am. Most firms have a two-and-twenty fee structure, which means they get a 2 percent management fee from their investors and then a 20 percent performance fee on the money they make from their deals. So if you're working with someone who doesn't really have your best interests at heart, you can get screwed, big time.

Sometimes it's obvious that the owner of the fund isn't in the business of making you money. Take, for example, Kim Kardashian (and you thought I was finished with the horror show part of the chapter). Yes, the Kardashians have ventured into the world of finance. In September 2022, Kim launched her own PE firm … with the help of Jay Sammons, a former partner at the Carlyle Group, a global investment company with about $370 billion in assets.[88] The Carlyle Group's leadership team is comprised of twenty-one men and ten women.[89]

---

88 "Kim Kardashian launches private equity firm." *The Guardian*. September 8, 2022. https://www.theguardian.com/business/2022/sep/08/kim-kardashian-launch-private-equity-firm-carlyle-skky-partners Accessed December 1, 2022.
89 https://www.carlyle.com/ Accessed December 2, 2022.

Kardashian announced her new firm, called SKKY Partners, will be making investments in minority companies and taking controlling stakes in "high-growth, market-leading consumer and media companies."[90] Now why would she want to do that? Am I being too cynical, or would she maybe want to become an influencer in new ways, such as by destroying companies that are her competitors and directing media companies to promote her businesses? Besides which, considering she's a social media queen, just think what one Tweet can do to stock prices. And no matter what happens to the companies she's investing in, she'll be getting 2 percent of her investors' money.

And Kardashian (and her mom, who is listed as a partner) are not the only celebrities getting into the game. LeBron James, Magic Johnson, Serena Williams, and Will Smith also started PE firms in 2022, and likely not for the social good or even the good of the companies in which they'll invest the funds. Although Kim claims she's got the business acumen to use her fund dollars to help founders raise their companies to an entirely new level, other celebrities typically seek out struggling companies for leveraged buyouts. In a leveraged buyout (LBO), PE fund managers buy the near-dead company, load it up with debt, overhaul its business, then sell it or take it public. The rub is that in about 20 percent of cases, the company ends up going bankrupt, like in the case of "Toys R Us." Even though Toys R Us is currently coming back from the grave, its 2018 bankruptcy put 30,000 employees out of work. I don't know about you, but I don't want any part in that.

It's not like I'm the first to point this out. According to Johns Hopkins University Carey Business School Professor Jeffrey Hooke, some fund managers are just tantalized by high fees. "[PE has] survived by being secretive

90 *The Guardian,* op cit.

and by perpetuating a myth that it's providing great returns to investors."[91] It isn't always. Also, as recently stated in a report from *Mother Jones*, many PE firms will do worse than feast on the dying like vultures; they will also "stalk and gut healthy ones."[92] If you have a conscience, you have to be careful. As Warren Buffet would tell you, knowing the people is important.

You will hear horror stories of what happened to somebody's grandmother after PE bought up the nursing home, the sorry care someone got after PE grabbed their general practitioner's practice, and the devastation in neighborhoods when PE buys up the housing stock. Those stories are real.

But that's just one more reason why you should know where your money is going, and with whom. You need to trust the fund manager as much as you trust your dentist. You do not want to create new pain for yourself while out there building security.

There's enough pain in the world already. We don't need to add to it by squandering opportunities to become independent and strong. We can do better than Wall Street, and we do. We can invest in companies and industries we believe in and are proud to support. We can do better things, and we can do better ourselves.

But first, to quote Kim kardashian-**"get your f------ ass up and work"**, and pay attention to opportunities people like me can help you find. Creativity applied by private equity can and does drive sustainable long-term growth, no matter what's going on with the Dow Jones. We

91 Morrow, Alison. "Why celebrities are so interested in the unglamorous world of private equity." CNN.com. September 7, 2022. https://www.cnn.com/2022/09/07/business/nightcap-kim-kardashian-private-equity Accessed December 1, 2022.
92 Ibid.

outperform finicky traditional investments, and you get the opportunity to watch your wealth grow and companies innovate and thrive.

The best PE firms have sophisticated teams with deep industry knowledge and operating and management experience dedicated to improving the companies they invest in. They care about you and your money, are happy to answer any questions, and respect your reservations. Companies like that—like mine—drive growth through excellence in sales, improved operations, and investing in technology and new products, which, in turn, revolutionize marketing.

Good PE firms succeed when the companies in which they invest thrive. And when you invest in a company like that, you thrive, too.

About the Author

Kelly Ann Winget is the Founder of the Dallas-based private equity company, Alternative Wealth Partners (AWP). The daughter of a fifth-generation oil and gas family with assets in Louisiana, Oklahoma, and Texas, Kelly Ann has over a decade of experience in the alternative investment space sourcing creative capital for startups, oil and gas companies, manufacturing ventures, real estate, and several other emerging markets on behalf of high net worth and high-income clients. Over her career, she has successfully raised almost $1 billion in private capital for private placement opportunities, averaging 3-5X returns. She formed AWP in 2020 to offer clients the best of what the private market can offer.

Kelly Ann offers investors the opportunity to diversify their portfolio with private equity funds which is for accredited investors who are looking for a diversified portfolio of alternative, tax-advantaged, and high-yielding investments. The funds allow investors to own their own share of individual assets across more than five industries; their focuses are on cash-flowing tangible assets and proven private equity opportunities for growth.

Kelly Ann is a partner and speaker with Diversity Crew, an organization focused on providing corporate diversity, equity, and inclusion programming while improving bottom-line results.

Kelly Ann lives in Texas with her wife and two children, two big dogs and a cat that runs the house. Kelly and her wife, Sarah, enjoy traveling the world (especially France where they were engaged and married), "*instagrammable*" margaritas, and any trendy new restaurant. Kelly and Sarah are currently working together on a nonprofit helping women and families navigate their lives after experiencing trauma and/or economic hardship.

Pitch the Bitch is Kelly Ann's first book.

Connect with Kelly Ann at www.kellyannwinget.com or www.alternativewealthpartners.com

Instagram: https://www.instagram.com/kellyannwinget/

TikTok: https://www.tiktok.com/@kellyannwinget